DIGITAL IRREVERENT

URIEL JAROSLAWSKI

PASSIONPRENEUR® PUBLISHING

DIGITAL IRREVERENT

How techies triumph over authority

URIEL JAROSLAWSKI

PASSIONPRENEUR®
PUBLISHING

Digital Irreverent
Copyright © 2024 Uriel Jaroslawski
First published in 2024

Print: 978-1-76124-199-4
E-book: 978-1-76124-201-4
Hardback: 978-1-76124-200-7

Because of the dynamic nature of the Internet, any web addresses or links contained in this book may have changed since publication and may no longer be valid. The information in this book is based on the author's experiences and opinions. The views expressed in this book are solely those of the author and do not necessarily reflect the views of the publisher; the publisher hereby disclaims any responsibility for them.

The author of this book does not dispense any form of medical, legal, financial, or technical advice either directly or indirectly. The intent of the author is solely to provide information of a general nature to help you in your quest for personal development and growth. In the event you use any of the information in this book, the author and the publisher assume no responsibility for your actions. If any form of expert assistance is required, the services of a competent professional should be sought.

Publishing information
Publishing and design facilitated by Passionpreneur Publishing
A division of Passionpreneur Organization Pty Ltd
ABN: 48640637529

Melbourne, VIC | Australia
www.passionpreneurpublishing.com

To my wife, who supported me every day in this adventure while starting her entrepreneurial journey. She is my sparring partner, with whom I test challenging ideas and explore different worldviews.

To my mother, who always taught me to think big and exemplified courage.

To my sister, an unstoppable force of nature: my role model for discipline and determination.

To my aunt, an incredible, insightful individual, who inspires me with her achievements and resilience. She encouraged me to commence this writing journey during our trip to Nepal.

TABLE OF CONTENTS

ACKNOWLEDGMENTS

I feel immensely privileged for the career opportunities I had, having worked with outstanding people at MELI, Quicko, Swvl, and Edenred. I borrowed many ideas from all the leaders I worked with, but I'm especially thankful for those who trusted my coaching: they were courageous enough to change things and kept multiplying this impact in their own paths.

TESTIMONIALS

Uriel's vision and leadership were fundamental to Quicko: by promoting a true transformation in the product and technology teams, Uriel made the platform more useful and relevant to our customers, enabling exponential growth in the following years. I'm glad he has decided to share his insights with the rest of the world!

—PEDRO SOMMA
(CEO AT BETTHA)

Meeting Uriel at Mercado Libre, after selling my first tech startup, marked a pivotal moment in my leadership journey. He was a guiding force in my transition to a leader of tech leaders. Under his mentorship, I refined critical skills in recruitment, motivation, retention, and organizing teams effectively. Uriel's expertise in establishing meaningful team rituals, efficient processes, and targeted training was instrumental. He also opened my eyes to the importance of moving tech professionals beyond the realm of coding. By engaging them in the broader business context, he showed me how to unlock their full potential. These lessons from Uriel have been invaluable; they reshaped my approach to team management and contributed greatly to my success in selling another tech startup and in starting my third venture. Witnessing Uriel's career flourish is a testament to the depth of his expertise and leadership skills. His journey is not just inspiring but also a valuable learning source for anyone aspiring to elevate their role in tech team leadership.

—FERNANDO MONTERA
(CEO AND CO-FOUNDER AT DOJI)

FOREWORD

First impressions matter. My encounter with Uriel on the 2nd of June 2022, in my Dubai office, was no exception.

After our 50-minute meeting, I knew he was special.

He was not only calm and collected, radiating clear thinking and discipline, he embodied the qualities we sought in our CTO. Respectful, cheerful, humble, knowledgeable, energetic, entrepreneurial, full of imagination as well as passion for customers.

The excitement was palpable, and I rushed to our Director of HR, declaring: 'We need him tomorrow. We've found our gem!'

True to his character, Uriel didn't immediately settle into a corner office. Instead, he chose the smallest desk in the open area, surrounding himself with Engineers, Product Managers, and Marketers of all levels. This wasn't just a location choice; it was a message: **humility, capability, and accessibility**.

Uriel's infectious energy and methodical thinking are matched only by his remarkable technical expertise. But what truly sets him apart is his ability to connect with people. He motivates, trains, and holds them accountable with a unique blend of wisdom and genuine understanding. He cuts through complexity with relatable stories and possesses an uncanny ability to connect with every individual in the office.

From our Friday afternoon one-on-ones to the weekly leadership meetings on Tuesdays, and even strategy sessions on a boat in El Gouna, Egypt, Uriel has consistently enriched our life and leadership journey. He's not just a colleague; he's a friend, mentor, and teacher who's impacted us all in so many profound ways.

Over the last two years, I've gotten to know more about Uriel (the person and the professional). He possesses a rare blend of seemingly contradictory strengths. He's calm and sharp, soft-spoken yet firm, serious yet doesn't take himself too seriously. Since joining, he's become a beacon of inspiration, innovation, and wisdom, not just for our leadership team but for the entire company, both inside and outside the UAE.

Having read the first draft of this book, I have no doubt it will resonate with many. It reflects the wisdom and knowledge that Uriel embodies—a treasure trove of technical brilliance and human compassion. More than just a book, it's a testament to Uriel's journey, and countless others will benefit from its insights.

With much admiration and respect,
Wael Fakharany
CEO Middle East, Edenred - March 2024

INTRODUCTION

In 2023, as I write this book, there are more than 60 million digital professionals worldwide. I estimate that less than three million of them work for the few companies that dominate the demand-driven economy, or those that share the same innovative mindset to a greater or lesser degree. More concretely, these companies probably developed the top five applications you use every day. Although I didn't realize the importance of the statement at the time, I was privileged to contribute to the success story of one of these companies in Latin America, whose working culture was quite different from that of most organizations. I believe that part of this difference acted as a key for unlocking most of the exponential impact we've witnessed during the last few decades in the digital space: 'irreverence' is the term I've coined to describe this key (i.e. the divergent work culture). The 'digital irreverence' idea negates the mandate to respect authorities or things, such as titles or companies, when they don't encourage people to produce the right impact. By removing power from unnecessary authorities—real or symbolic—and from the status quo, we unlock the potential for curiosity and a sense of ownership; thus, we can overcome complex challenges and make decisions that get to the heart of the problems. Irreverent teams are unbeatable in ambiguous scenarios because they mitigate environmental uncertainty as part of their work and adapt quickly.

I dedicated most of my career to transforming how some of the remaining 57 million digital professionals work (i.e., the 95% who probably never considered working completely autonomously or becoming decision-makers in the business they played a role in building).

On one particular day in 2023, I was preparing slides for a lean product management training for my team, and realized that I was going to repeat the same story that I'd been telling my previous teams in different parts of the world for years. That's when I decided to write this book: I understood that my mission is to scale the impact of the 95% by introducing a different approach to product development and leadership.

I can't tell you that I was once in your place. Most likely, I wasn't. I was one of the few people who 'boarded a rocket ship' during the internet boom—one of the probably ten or twenty in the world that departs every generation. Although my former company's working style was quite differentiated, it became normal for me and set the bar at a point where I couldn't accept compromising on culture. I, therefore, continued enhancing my skills over the years to effect the change I wanted to witness in other companies. I can confidently tell you that I understand the frustration of being disconnected from the meaning of your work and its impact. I drove transformations from 'the other side of the shore', enabling many people and teams to perceive things differently in the digital space. In doing so, I helped them overcome constraints imposed by the industrial mindset, which formerly dominated their workplace.

In the late 1950s, S&P 500 companies lived three times longer than those in the same index in 2010. What changed in six decades?

SUPPLY-DRIVEN OR DEMAND-DRIVEN

The companies operating in the late 1950s were founded in the Industrial Age; consequently, they possessed an industrial mindset. Industries immensely upscaled production to levels not witnessed in the handicraft era: they utilized machinery and technology, and they simplified the work of individuals to match the minimum level of learning needed. That type of work was measured in hours. Because it was a commodity, with the right capital you could purchase technology and machinery, and pay workers for their hours of work. Therefore, when a company with capital offered the right product to the market and was supported by the right political or economic impetus to dominate distribution, it benefited from a virtuous cycle referred to as economies of scale; thus, the company gained efficiency, reduced costs, and exhibited capital gain, which enabled it to keep expanding and feed the same cycle.

This represented a supply-driven economy where an individual or company could have a strong influence on a particular market if they had the proper scale, capital, and distribution. In a supply-driven economy, you succeed when you enhance the efficiency of processes, minimize costs, control quality, and optimize distribution. The capital growth derived from this optimization even enables you to acquire companies in different geographies; their operations can then be optimized in the same manner as that of the acquiring company.

In this type of economy, we respond to authorities and ideas such as quality in the processes, efficiency, managers, company owners, investors, and regulators.

When we analyze the S&P 500 companies in 2010, it's apparent that technology-based companies are quite dominant. What happens when you sell digital products and services in 2010? That was the year when US smartphone penetration exceeded 25%, defining an exponential curve that would propel it above 80% in only five years. The other exponential curve that was being defined that year was that of cloud computing. After Amazon Web Services was launched in 2006 and Microsoft Azure Cloud in 2010, most of the world started shifting from on-premises data centers to cloud computing. This $24.6 billion market in 2010 was on its way to exceeding $100 billion seven years later. Smartphone penetration, together with services such as search engines, social media, and mobile app stores, offered a cheap and accessible distribution channel for almost any digital product. Meanwhile, cloud computing, combined with more evolved software development technologies, equipped almost anyone with the ability to develop applications and distribute them online without having to invest in data centers or expensive technology infrastructure, which was the only option just a few years before these technologies became widely available.

As it became easier to build and distribute digital products and services, we transitioned to a demand-driven economy.

In a demand-driven economy, the consumer has the strongest influence on how the market operates. A social media platform can become irrelevant in a matter of months if its network externalities are weakened, with users fleeing just by downloading a new app. On the user side, the cost of switching can be quite low depending on the network's strength.

In these economies, the capital you own, the quality of your processes, or the products you manage to build are inconsequential; what matters most is whether they're connected to what the customer really needs. This idea has always been true in a free market. However, since around 2010, companies haven't had enough time to react if this sense of connection wasn't part of their organization's DNA.

The topmost authority in a demand-driven economy is the customer, and this context is what creates a VUCA (volatile, uncertain, chaotic, and ambiguous) environment, where the nature of the talent you possess in your workforce can no longer be a commodity. For every opportunity presented by a digital product, there are several possible solutions, and each solution has many ways of being implemented technically. Each combination of decisions leads to an outcome—and to optimize for the right outcome, you need people who can effectively collaborate with an interdisciplinary approach, coupled with a good understanding of what they are working for and what their context is.

How many times can I ask you why you're doing what you're doing at work before you refer to an authority who defines this for you?

I couldn't ask most people this more than once or twice before they referred to a boss or to another person in their team who defines what they do at some level. We're trying to succeed in building products and services in a dynamic environment. It's part of our nature to try to stay in a safe space where responsibilities and ownership can be perfectly divided and assigned; however, this space doesn't really exist in competitive economies.

The real success stories in the Digital Age are a little bit messier: the imaginary safe space that we perceive in many teams is nonexistent, and successful companies are a lot more authentic in their understanding of impact and their connection with purpose. This is what I term the *irreverent way.* In this book, I equip readers with an understanding of the difference between the safe, industrial-minded way and the irreverent way. I won't teach you a methodology with predefined names for every role that pretentiously enables you to deliver projects quicker; instead, I'll provide you with a framework with which you can work towards a first-principles approach that puts your customers and your company's impact at the center while excluding outdated authorities. Thus, beyond the production of tangible results at work, it will also nourish a seed of authenticity for fulfillment and enjoyment in your career.

CHAPTER 1

THE IRREVERENT JOURNEY

BUENOS AIRES

2005

I was taking the elevator down from the eighth to the sixth floor of Mercado Libre's offices. It was an afternoon in the third week of September. That was the first week of my internship at Mercado Libre (a.k.a. Meli), and I was really proud of the notes I'd taken from my meeting with Mache (my first business stakeholder), who was leading the Supply team in the marketplace business.

Although I felt confident about my technical skills and problem-solving ability, I'd never dealt with stakeholders or analyzed problems at this scale. However, I knew I could meet Mache's requirements. After all, that's what engineering is all about—at least that's what I was taught at university. There's always going to be a businessperson or somebody else who defines the *What*, which then leaves you to figure out the *How*. You know how to build things. However, somebody else knows what they need for their organization, and this understanding is what's going to be required.

The next day, I met Soko (my CTO at the time) on the sixth floor, who wanted to know how I was doing. He asked me how my meeting with Mache went, what we were going to do about supply, and to state the initiatives that we should be working on.

In response, I took out my notes and started explaining what the requirements were and how I was initially planning to build a specific tool. He then looked at me and asked why. I replied, 'What do you mean by "Why"?' He insisted, 'Yes, why should we build this? Why are you working on this?' His tone indicated that he didn't think I was doing something wrong; he was merely focusing on the 'Why'.

We were trying to build a tool for detecting high-potential sellers in the marketplace, as the e-commerce penetration in Latin America was nascent. By identifying the early adopters and fast-growing sellers, we could utilize resources in such a way as to accelerate the network effect.

Although that was important, I was ignorant of *why* we needed to build a tool to detect high-potential sellers. The requirements I'd written probably made sense; however, I had no way of explaining why we were building the tool or why it was crucial, neither could I list alternative approaches to the same problem. Consequently, I did what most people do when these types of questions arise: I referred to an authority, informing my CTO that Mache was the one who defined this, and he was the one who knew what we needed. Fortunately for my career and for the growth of e-commerce in the region, that answer wasn't accepted at Meli, especially if you were working in our Engineering team. You needed to know why (i.e., to understand the 'Why', to own it, and to be accountable for each decision)—even if it wasn't a technical decision.

Our team, which consisted of fewer than thirty Engineers, had already learned this lesson well. We called ourselves the Product team, even though there were no official Product Managers for a few years. As Engineers, our understanding of the business, of the product itself, and of everything else around Meli empowered us to move really quickly as we scaled; however, I had no idea that this was a competitive advantage. Our situation reminds me of the story of the fish who meets another fish in the pond and comments, 'The water's great today,' and the other fish replies, 'What's water?'

2007: IRREVERENT BEGINNINGS

After Meli's IPO, we accelerated hiring, especially for Engineering, and acquired different companies in Latin America. Although I was overly engaged with the technical challenges we faced, and felt quite confident about our ability to collaborate as a team, this new stage implied that many of us had to step up and assume leadership roles. Careerwise, that's usually a very exciting moment for anyone; but when the stakes are higher—for example, when new leaders are joining from different countries and backgrounds, wishing to drive impact without necessarily being used to our way of working—some more complex stakeholder management is needed.

How do you challenge a senior business leader's decision when you're a 20-something-year-old recent graduate, who can't necessarily articulate the business logic of why you believe we should do something differently to what a particular person says?

In one of these attempts, I heard one of the most heart-breaking phrases an Engineer at Meli could hear. There's a saying in Spanish translated as 'shoemaker to your shoes', which means 'take care of your part of the work' or 'mind your own business', depending on the context. It's no coincidence that I still remember that phrase today.

Dani, our new CTO, who was previously working as an Engineering Manager when I joined Meli, was determined to maintain the right company culture as we scaled, especially when we discussed the Engineering team. Every quarter he was communicating strategy, the initiatives we were working on, and how the business was going in general; furthermore, he always provided key messages about what he expected from us. In one of those presentations, I heard for the first time—in a work-based context—the word *irreverent*.

He was saying that to succeed in the Meli Engineering team, you are required to be irreverent. Although he didn't care to break down that explanation to make it more explicit, I understood what it meant—at least intuitively. I didn't reflect deeply on that idea until later in my career.

What Dani meant at that time was a combination of not accepting the status quo and having the drive to fight any authority-based bias. Both implied having the courage to speak up and to ask 'why' when we need to. If at some point we struggled while deciding something together with other business leaders and we couldn't easily align, Dani wouldn't hesitate to jump in and participate with us. He made it look easy. He was very clear on the big picture and how we needed to work; therefore, the alignment happened every time. Although this doesn't mean that he was always right, his clarity of mind and drive were enough to help us move forward. Of course, after these interventions, Dani expected us to take charge and become our own version of the Engineering leaders Meli needed.

IMPACT BEYOND TECHNOLOGY

I ended up spending part of my Engineering Management time learning about product management, benchmarking competitors, learning more about the business, and understanding different models and how they worked in different countries among other things. The skills I developed made me feel quite empowered, which was a key element for my career growth and motivated me more than the technical challenges. I worked on five mergers and acquisitions, leading the technical integrations; every time, I was surprised by the gap between our working style and that of the other company. Although this didn't prevent me learning many things from each of these experiences and from the teams I had to work with, every single time, the decision-making power of the people who were actually building the product was nearly zero.

In most scenarios, the technology, user experience, and product management were commodities. Although there was a business requirement and somebody with a vision that was actualized through technology, these teams in themselves had very little say in what they were building. These cases were characterized by an accumulation of technical debt and the existence of legacy systems very few people knew how to maintain, and there were implied risks that some leaders weren't even aware of. Through each of these experiences, I became 'the fish who had to leave the pond every once in a while to look back and realize the water condition'. I calibrated my understanding of the working style that made us unique at Meli, perfecting my methods over time to enable new teams to join the irreverent club.

I failed miserably in some cases, but learned new things each time; I did this in Brazil, Mexico, Chile, and Venezuela, gaining many insights into the underlying culture of each country, company, and founder that shaped people's behavior and working style.

Meanwhile, each of these companies ended up teaching us crucial lessons aimed at improving our business, including customer experience, sales, and PR. I learned to face any new integration or transformation with more humility each time. This enabled me not only to improve the tools I was building to make these transformations, but also to create relationships that outlived my time at Meli—today, many of the people I worked with are my friends.

WELCOME TO BRAZIL

In 2018, I took up the challenge to lead the Developer Relationships team for the Marketplace business in Brazil, which entailed assisting hundreds of startups and larger companies to develop applications and integrations for sellers. This was the least technical role I've ever assumed in my career; however, it gave me a lot of insight into how products that people use every day were being developed by startups and larger corporations that were integrated with our marketplace. This role gave me the opportunity to intervene and enable them to perceive product development in a different manner.

Meli was almost becoming the most valuable company in Latin America, and with the evidence I'd gathered from the outside world, it was apparent that I could make a bigger difference in another company or team. This era was characterized by a lot of booming startups in Brazil and a market thirsty for digital talent.

I also wanted to prove that I could build high-performing teams outside of Meli, especially with more challenging conditions and a different talent budget than Meli could offer. Contrary to the recommendations of family and friends, which indicated that the risk of regret after leaving such a remarkable company was high, I joined Quicko as the CTO on the same day the app was launched. It was a corporate venture: an early-stage startup aimed at improving urban mobility and access to public transportation in Brazil through technology. The previous CTO and the Chief Product Officer had both resigned in the course of the previous four months; therefore, the CEO was glad to give me the freedom to assume both roles.

This was my time to redefine how to build an irreverent team. The business context was extremely challenging, especially after the pandemic; this condition provided me with the 'sandbox' I needed to experiment with building a potentially successful product from scratch, and also how to build a high-performing team based on the principles I'd experienced. This experiment worked. I'd built—for the first time—a team from scratch. I'd matured at Meli, and was applying the principles I'd learnt; as a result, people were quickly increasing their impact. We witnessed great improvements in the business despite the challenging conditions, and Quicko got acquired in early 2022 by a European company operating in the mobility space.

Owing to the financial risks of this business and challenging market conditions that the year 2022 presented to every startup worldwide, Quicko ended its ride in 2023; however, that was undoubtedly one of my most fulfilling career experiences, where I could materialize my own approach to digital product development.

I raised the bet that year and decided to relocate to the Middle East by joining a promising mobility startup based in Egypt. They were trying to transform the way they worked and upscale as a global platform. When I say that I raised the bet, I'm not referring to technical challenges. It was all about people: a cultural challenge. This ambitious startup was on the verge of undergoing an IPO, and until just months before I joined, almost all of the engineering work was being done in the Cairo offices. Suddenly, the team had to start collaborating with a Dubai-based Product team, where most of the people were from India.

CULTURAL STRETCHING

As you can imagine, I couldn't miss such an adventure. This company, which was named Swvl, was the first Egyptian unicorn (the first startup valued at $1 billion founded in that country) and was built by a team of hustlers. Although they'd gradually incorporated some good practices and methodology, the highest value of all was the resilience and trust they built within the team. The Product Managers in Dubai were very practical. In most scenarios, they were also quite agreeable towards authority figures. They usually felt overwhelmed when their interactions with their Egyptian colleagues were filled with emotions and frustrations about decisions that weren't understood by everyone in the same way. At the end of the day, everyone was working very hard, but they weren't necessarily optimizing for the same outcome. This evidenced one of the most critical learnings in my career.

The caliber of talent you have in your team won't matter if you don't share the same definition of success. Two months after its IPO, Swvl had a funding setback that forced it to lay off most of its team worldwide and resort to utilizing a small Engineering team in Cairo.

Even if this experience lasted only a few months, it opened my eyes to a new world. The lessons that I'd learned and taught in Latin America weren't directly applicable in this region. I was unemployed in Dubai for eight days until I joined Edenred, a French-born company that grew to become the largest player in the employee benefits and engagement industry worldwide. In the UAE, Edenred was doing something different: it was working on a payroll program driven as a FinTech, providing digital financial tools for migrant workers in the country. I nearly canceled my first interview at Edenred because I was quite skeptical of joining a large corporation. Although I preferred start-ups, in my early interviews, I discovered this wasn't the old-fashioned corporation I'd imagined. Even if it was a huge global company, it operated in a multi-local manner. This meant that every operation and business unit worked with a high level of empowerment and made decisions locally, while leveraging the strengths of the global brand and the talent synergies.

The state of Edenred's Engineering team in the UAE wasn't much better than what I'd witnessed ten years before in my M&A experiences in Mexico, Venezuela, Chile, and Brazil. Even when some things seemed apparent to many leaders in our industry, I approached this challenge with great humility. Although this was another blank page, this time I decided to document every step. I wanted to facilitate the replication of this transformation not only for my teams, but for other people, who could then use these learnings in other places and with other teams.

In a very short time, we managed to grow the penetration of different financial services on our C3Pay app and create new products that accelerated financial inclusion.

The team learned to work in an experimentation-driven manner, where everyone could connect what they were doing with every single company goal. When I look back on my career, even if I could list many business achievements, the highest reward of all is witnessing the personal growth of the people I'd led, how they began perceiving things in a way they hadn't before, and how this enabled them to ignite their own personal transformation. At the end of the day, the story of the irreverent is also a story of fulfillment—of feeling satisfied with the work you do every day.

HIERARCHY AND NEEDS

When we look back at satisfaction at work in the industrial-minded world, most of the work is mechanized and commoditized. People are referred to as resources, and their leaders calculate their productivity based on the hourly rate and measurable outputs; however, that mindset is incompatible with a digital organization. When you build two parallel teams where team members on both sides have equivalent years of experience in the same fields, technically, you can't identify any difference between Team A and Team B. In this scenario, will the outcomes be equal? In the digital world, that's never the case. There are so many more variables that affect this equation: you can't measure that efficiency in terms of hours and the number of workers. Although you can calculate financial efficiency over a period of time, this metric isn't a predictor of success in the digital world. How the team collaborates, their aversion to risk, their curiosity, and their motivation level all play key roles in achieving the right outcomes.

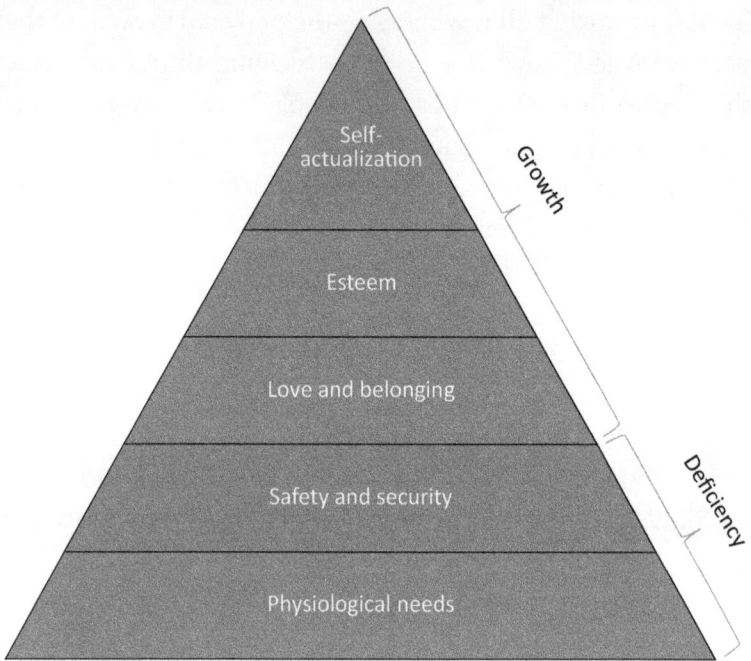

In 1954, American psychologist Abraham Maslow created a model for explaining individuals' hierarchy of needs. He defines two groups of needs:

1. the deficiency needs
2. the growth needs.

He then defined the five-level pyramid:

- The lowest and widest layer comprises the physiological needs, such as air, water, food, and shelter.
- The second layer refers to safety needs, including personal security, employment, health, property, and resources.

- The third layer is based on needs related to belonging and love, including intimate relationships and friends.
- The fourth layer refers to esteem needs, which relate to self-esteem, where you recognize a sense of prestige or accomplishment.
- The two aforementioned layers are considered psychological needs.
- The fifth and last level is self-actualization, which is related to achieving one's potential, including creative activities and work connected with a sense of purpose.

So, how is Maslow's Hierarchy of Needs Pyramid related to the comparison between the Industrial Age and the Digital Age?

In the Industrial Age, most people were working to fulfil their deficiency needs. While the scarce technical talent we need to succeed in the Digital Age entails looking for something beyond safety, this also generates the right virtuous cycle, where the right team with the right skills and a clear purpose can achieve remarkable things. Thus, work shouldn't be treated as a commodity.

I consider work and talent distribution in the industrial companies asymmetrical, which indicates that the distances in terms of intellectual complexity between disciplines, seniority levels, or departments are of different orders of magnitude: they belong to a different scale. We can utilize the simplified example of a Medical team where a doctor is performing a surgery and a nurse is assisting the patient. In that relationship, there's a clear difference of authority: one person knows much more than the other in that field of expertise. In the digital space, most teams are built of symmetrical talent. A Product Designer isn't expecting a Software Engineer to tell her the right way of doing her job: both are specialized in their own fields. The difference in expertise is unrelated to a difference in hierarchy.

However, one of the things that *hasn't* changed since the Industrial Age is that we still create authorities between these teams—calling some people owners or managers or heads of certain processes. It's this behavior that transforms a symmetrical relationship by nature into an asymmetrical relationship.

The bottom line is, the only way your company or your organization can live long enough in the digital world is by building symmetrical teams with a high sense of collaboration, motivated by a purpose, with a strong customer focus, and empowered enough to be able to adapt to any circumstances.

MY BELIEFS

1. For most companies, the tangible and intangible authorities they reverence today were inherited from the Industrial Age. Moving from the supply-driven economy, where many industrial-minded companies succeeded, to the demand-driven economy, which rules the market in the Digital Age, the ability to adapt quickly, understand your customers' needs, and satisfy these needs are crucial for

survival. Which authorities do you respect that are limiting your ability to adapt quickly?

2. To build the right solutions to the right needs within a competitive timeframe, decisions should be made as close to the problem as possible. Empowered, interdisciplinary, and symmetrical teams are most likely to achieve this outcome. Building successful digital products isn't possible through commoditized work; motivated individuals driven by purpose make the difference. What are the unnecessary hierarchies that exist in your team?

3. People that are new to your industry aren't conditioned by the legacy authorities: they'll help you challenge the status quo, and catch up with the required knowledge in a matter of months or weeks if they have the right learning agility. Because different cultures shape the authorities' landscape differently, having a diverse team can maximize the chances of identifying your blind spots. How can you check your team's authority-related biases?

CHAPTER 2

NEED FOR IRREVERENCE

Why do most Product Development teams fail?

Nubank, a digital native bank, was funded in Brazil in 2013 to drive financial inclusion in the region. That was the year when the Brazilian population exceeded 200 million people, 40% of whom were unbanked. Nubank started offering a debit card and a free digital account to people regardless of their income level; their customer support merits a case study. Nubank intentionally built a Leadership team with people from different countries, making sure most of them didn't come from the banking industry. In 2023, they became the fourth-largest bank in Brazil, and had expanded to countries such as Mexico and Argentina: a level of growth that no legacy bank has achieved, regardless of the investment they dedicated to their digital wing.

The reason this company was intentionally hiring people from other industries with less experience in the finance world was because they needed to disrupt the country's banking system by creating a team of 'irreverents'. Although they respect regulations, they don't accept that a bank should have branches or ATMs; even though they respect the Central Bank, they don't respect the monetization models of the banks in the region.

Without a doubt, what Nubank respects most is their customers. By hiring outsiders, they organically created a symmetrical team without a sense of reverence to the pre-existing authorities. Why did I care to mention that most leaders were coming from different countries? I don't know if this idea was considered by Nubank's founders; although the founders were probably already in an international context when they decided to be partners in this endeavor, I want to highlight the implications of our countries', families', and communities' cultures in the decisions we make every day and the authorities we respect. These influences strike a better balance when we create diverse teams.

One of my favorite books is *Outliers* by Malcolm Gladwell, which has a chapter dedicated to understanding plane crashes from a cultural and ethnic-based perspective. Gladwell shares transcripts of the Black Boxes of plane crashes from Korean Air and Avianca (the Colombian airline). In every case, there's a First Officer who's aware of challenging conditions pertaining to a specific problem: something that's going wrong. However, he doesn't address this point with the Captain in a direct or clear manner. Their sense of reverence towards the Captain overcomes any impulse to save their own lives or save the plane with its passengers. You may even think that these scenarios are ridiculous and that something like this would never happen to you: that you'd probably react. You'd tell the captain to do something, or you'd shout to get his or her attention—no matter his or her authority. However, the reality is that most of us carry along some conditioning from our cultural and family background.

There's some authority that we respect in a non-rational way. Is there anybody from work, from school, or from your family that you dare not say 'no' to? Is there somebody whose opinion you dare not challenge?

I've cited the book *Outliers* to demonstrate that there are cultures where reverences are more deeply rooted. This isn't an excuse for you to discriminate against people based on nationality or culture. It's the reason diversity can be considered one of the key elements of the irreverent team, which tries to be conscious of its cultural influences.

How can this be applied to your current job? Do you think your company has what it takes to achieve longevity? In this Digital Age, how do you adapt to a demand-driven economy by navigating the irreverent way?

THE DEFINITION OF IRREVERENT

Let's begin with a more objective definition of the term 'irreverent': 'Having or showing a lack of respect for someone or something that is usually treated with respect.'

What is it that's usually treated with respect in our working context? Do we respect our CEO, our investors, people around us who bear the title *manager*? Do we respect regulations? Do we respect customers? Do we respect budgets? Do we respect business plans?

I'm not suggesting that you should lose respect for everyone or everything around you. I'm challenging you to lose respect for the things which, while commanding respect in our business world, negatively contribute to the results we seek.

Another familiar context where you can encounter the word 'irreverent' is when some people refer to a child not behaving well. Some children are called irreverent when they ask what they *shouldn't* be asking: for example, when they're told to do something and then ask why. Maybe challenging their parents is entertaining, or maybe, in some scenarios, the child is genuinely curious: they simply want to understand the Why.

The adult world taught us to eliminate that curiosity as a means of surviving in society: to know the rules, the authorities, and how we should respect them.

What if a curious child arrived at your workplace? Assume the child saw what you and other people are doing and how you're communicating with each other. Imagine that this child was genuinely curious about why things are as they seem. Imagining this situation can be quite an insightful exercise for gaining a perspective on the things that don't necessarily make sense. I'm pretty sure that you've already identified things that should be different in the way you work.

The reality is that most people live in an illusion of separation, where responsibilities and scopes can be perfectly divided, and where each one of us is accountable for a specific thing. However, the truth is that when you're more connected with the complete scope, your decision-making ability increases. Most successful endeavors are reliant on people figuring out the right way of collaborating.

One of the things that frustrates me the most when we build digital products in some companies is when we decide to call teammates 'owners', thereby imposing (by definition) a lack of ownership by everybody else. I know there are amazing Product Analysts who were assigned the title 'Product Owners'. If you're one of them, you most likely haven't graduated with a bachelor's degree in Product Ownership. Regardless of your degrees or major, you probably developed sharp problem-solving and stakeholder management skills. However, in a competitive digital market, you'll never be able to define (with the right level of detail) what somebody else in your team should be building. Every part of the technical work involves assumptions, and the only way to make the right ones is by making sure everyone involved has the right context and understanding of what you're doing and why; ideally, everyone should have the agency to decide what to do.

RETHINKING RESPECT

Let me offer an instructive example. When I joined Quicko in 2019, I asked one of the Mobile Engineers what solution they were using for the internationalization of texts in the app. I got no answer. Nobody in the Product team had proposed that we should support the app beyond Brazil. In a way, he was right: we had no intention of expanding beyond Brazil at that point. But at the same time, he'd made a definition (a product definition) that implied a big future endeavor if or when we decided to expand beyond Brazil. The problem wasn't the decision that was made; there was a low risk of that becoming an immediate problem. However, the fact is that a decision was arrived at, and nobody knew that it had been made.

Even when we have Product Owners or people with the word 'manager' in their job title (people who are responsible for defining what others should do), this will never be enough. Every part of the product you build contains multiple assumptions that must be made for things to work. Therefore, one of the things I'd like you to lose respect for is definitions or requirements that only derive from other teammates' interpretation of what should be done. I want you to lose respect for internal contracts that are built to make us feel safer, but in reality move us away from real success.

I mentioned internal contracts because if you're an external contractor, you'd probably be achieving success by selling more hours of work, and maybe that's okay. I still believe that in the long run, you can also be an irreverent in this case, and use this approach to achieve more sustainable success.

An example of internal contracts is the goals themselves—the objectives we set to measure our performance every year. Does everybody in the team have converging goals? Is everyone rewarded when we maximize the outcome that the company needs? Or are individuals rewarded by measuring progress in something that's not directly derived from the company's overall success?

A close relative to the illusion of separation is the illusion of control, which is when people believe they can control the outcomes by controlling the inputs, defining strict rules, and making sure everybody follows them.

Simon Sinek shared a story in one of his famous presentations: a particular barista, Noah, works in Las Vegas for the Four Seasons. He's performing amazingly well and being funny, and people like the work he does. Noah says he loves his job. He states that he also works at Caesar's Palace; this work is different, because his manager controls his work to ensure that he does things the right way. Noah performs much better in his job at the Four Seasons, because even the managers to whom he doesn't report directly are concerned about how they can support him instead of controlling him. The best version of this person's performance is shown when the least control is applied (when trust exists by default), and Noah can be himself at that job.

THE IRREVERENT FRAMEWORK

In the second half of 2018, I was leading the Developer Relations team for Mercado Libre's marketplace in Brazil. I quickly realized that the challenge was way beyond sensitizing some startups on how to develop their integration with us, or about providing any specific technical support. These companies deeply admired Meli, and considered us authorities in the digital space. A huge percentage of the marketplace sales were from sellers who were using these companies for their integrations, and there was a very close correlation between the quality of the integration and the sales. Therefore, we couldn't afford to let them perform only the technical part and ignore the rest. It was crucial that they also knew how to make the right product decisions.

In the first event I organized for the developer community, I took one of my presentation slots and got on stage to teach them about the lean product management approach. By that time, I already had accumulated many years of leading Engineering teams in the irreverent way; however, it was the first time I was teaching product management to other people, and the first time I had to study many of the topics I was willing to present. Even if I'd applied a big portion of that knowledge with my own teams, this was the first time I'd delved into its source.

This experience enabled me to confidently assume the Chief Product Officer and Chief Technology Officer roles when I joined Quicko in November 2019. That was the first time in my career I was building a product almost from scratch with no users, as well as trying to achieve product market fit with a completely new team. That was the perfect scenario to combine my irreverent approach to engineering leadership and my knowledge of lean product management as a means of creating a framework for a crucial transformation. Today, I call this framework the *Digital Irreverent Playbook*. This work has enabled me to improve the lives of hundreds of thousands of commuters in three major cities in Brazil using the Quicko app, which became the fastest-growing urban mobility app in the region at that time. Another impact related to applying the *Digital Irreverent Playbook* at Quicko was a career and personal transformation for Engineers, Product Managers,

Designers, and leaders who completely evolved the understanding of their roles in a team.

After this experience, I developed *The Digital Irreverent Playbook* further and expanded it into six steps. The next chapters are dedicated to each one of these steps.

Between 2022 and 2024, in my work as the CTO at Edenred in the UAE, I again applied these six steps; the transformation worked like clockwork.

In May of 2023, when I was preparing a presentation on the agile mindset, I realized that I should write a book on my playbook. I'm sharing this with you so that you too can find a path to agility that's not present in the typical frameworks we can identify in the industry.

The six steps of *The Digital Irreverent Playbook* are as follows:

1. Redefine success
2. Structure your team
3. Share ownership
4. Design feedback loops
5. Embrace uncertainty
6. Optimize learning cycles.

I'll discuss each one of these steps to give you a better idea of what they mean.

Redefine success is related to the question I asked in the beginning of the chapter: What are you optimizing for? The idea is to take a step back and ask the following: What *should* you optimize for? What does success mean for the company, for your team, and for you? In regard to redefining success, the crucial aspect is that you're always making a decision—whether you're conscious of it or not. In other words, if you can't clearly express what you're optimizing for and what success is for you, you're choosing to diverge from the real success. Once you take the step of defining success, the way you believe in it, and the way this belief is shared by the rest of your team and the company, all the remaining work becomes much easier. That's because you can cascade this broad concept into smaller definitions of success, which helps you align decisions in a much more effective way.

Structure your team is related to how you perceive talent in your organization. What is the minimum viable group of people collaborating with you that has the ability to build digital products in this irreverent way? What does it mean to build a team with symmetrical talent, and why does diversity play a key role in any irreverent team?

The third step, **share ownership**, comprises the core of the irreverent philosophy. It intends to eliminate authorities when they're not needed and is exemplified as follows: When we separate the definition of the work that *should* be done from the work itself. When one person defines something and the other person executes the definition, and when the success of the second person lies in executing whatever is defined, that's where we see an absence of shared ownership. In an irreverent team, nobody is rewarded for doing what the other person defined; however, individuals are rewarded for maximizing the chances of getting closer to what we collaboratively defined as success. This is the difference between optimizing locally and optimizing globally.

The fourth step, **design feedback loops**, attempts to define a very basic template of the most crucial conversations that should occur in an irreverent team. The irreverent team I envision rejects all forms of rigidly defined methodologies or practices that don't relate in an understandable way with the principles individuals believe in. The rituals I propose in this chapter are based on these principles; however, they can evolve, and will definitely do so over time.

The fifth step, **embracing uncertainty**, is based on the following idea: In a VUCA environment, it's misleading to assume certainty in how we prioritize efforts. I believe uncertainty should be a component of the equation indicating how we make decisions in every digital product. That doesn't mean you should focus your work on only the activities with high-level certainty, but that there is work you should do recurrently to reduce the uncertainty of the rest of the activities or to eliminate them.

Last, we discuss **learning cycles**. The more often you learn about what your users or customers really need, the easier it is for you to adapt as a means of achieving the success you defined as well as longevity. The learning process doesn't happen spontaneously. It happens by design. These processes should be managed, and they should be embedded in the team's culture. Many companies inherited the following misconception from industrial-minded leaders: mistakes should be punished. There's nothing more harmful for individuals' learning cycles than punishing mistakes. How do you manage performance in your team when you're optimizing for learning cycles? You should continuously learn about what you do and how you do it.

DON'T FALL IN LOVE WITH THE PROCESS

When we analyze the six steps, there's an intended chronology. However, that chronology isn't rigid: it can change. It's hard to succeed in this transformation if you don't define success in an appropriate way. It's also hard to succeed in embracing uncertainty if you don't have the right people in your team. Therefore, the real shape of this process resembles a spiral. You can execute the first layer of these six steps in a week or a month, and then you'll revisit each step. In my experience, the results of a transformation such as this are quite difficult to realize in less than eight to twelve months. Depending on the initial state of your company, your team, and the leadership, it will be perfectly natural to see people not embracing a high level of ownership, feeling insecure, and searching for clear definitions that resemble those they used to have.

You'll also see leaders losing power when the dynamic changes. Therefore, it's crucial to understand that the irreverent way isn't for everyone: not everyone should stay on board for the whole journey. However, the ones who stay have the chance to live the most fulfilling work experience by being able to connect their daily activities with purposeful and ambitious objectives. These people will never go back to working the way they used to because they'll see a different way that's effective and simple, while putting people at the center of things.

If you're ready for this journey, first identify what you're optimizing for and what success means to you.

CHAPTER 3

STEP 1:
REDEFINE SUCCESS

Optimize for the right outcomes

How do you define success? If you're working for a company or running your own business, you probably have a set of goals that you should meet in a certain timeframe to achieve an outcome that's intended to benefit this organization. It's also very likely that if these objectives are achieved or if this outcome is actualized, you'll be rewarded somehow.

The first problem we face in *The Digital Irreverent Playbook* is that many times you're not rewarded for the right thing or you're not optimizing for the right outcome. This could easily be related to an industrial mindset that believes that if we control the inputs, we'll be able to control the outputs. If the right inputs become the objectives, the right results become the output, and we can achieve success. It's like defining different objectives for buying the ingredients, and following the steps listed in a recipe to bake a cake. If you achieve each objective, you evidently bake a good cake, right?

Wrong.

When people try to bake that cake they saw in the recipe, even if they follow the steps correctly, they sometimes fail to arrive at the expected result. There are always many more variables that affect the process more significantly than the ones that can be accounted for in a recipe, a video, or any explanation by another person. In the case of the cake or in different cooking scenarios, you might need to practice until you achieve the expected result.

That's when you've successfully incorporated the variables you were missing, even if they were subtle or dependent on other contextual elements. This practice is usually what enables us to move from knowing to understanding. The cake example's equivalent in the product development world brings more layers of complexity that we should overcome. First, what do you need a cake for? Do you intend to sell the cake? Are you inviting friends over? Are you trying to impress someone with your baking abilities? In any case, what's the outcome you want to achieve, and how will you measure if and when you achieve it?

Let's suppose you want to impress two of your friends from your yoga class. Even if they don't know you that well (because you started yoga last month), you want to get invited to the retreat they're planning. You assume that having them over to your place and sharing a good cake you baked will win their hearts, and that they'll think it'll be a good idea to tell you about the trip and invite you. This trip invitation will be your success.

ESCALATION OF COMMITMENT

You plan to buy the following ingredients: milk, eggs, sugar, almond flour, and ripe bananas. To add a first layer of complexity, as we can imagine in the digital world, you're not in the same country as where the recipe's from. Consequently, you not only lack access to the brands that were recommended, but are also struggling to find almond flour in the supermarket you usually visit. What do you replace it with? You'll figure something out. The oven you're using isn't electric, as in the recipe. You, therefore, try to regulate the temperature in the best way possible.

You finish baking your banana cake, and it looks awful. You taste it, and you don't like it. But you still have a couple of hours, and if you buy some more ingredients you already know, you can probably have a better cake ready for when they arrive. So, you try this again. You bring home all the ingredients, check the mixture twice, then bake it at the right temperature; even if you're ten minutes late, this cake is apparently in much better shape than the last one. Your friends arrive, you entertain them with some tea, and they can already smell the cake being baked.

You're actually a coffee person, so the tea you gave them isn't great. They started comparing it with the organic brand everybody talks about in class, and yours is much worse. When you take the cake out of the oven, it's a little bit burnt. When you're slicing the cake, you taste a small slice and realize it's not too bad. You take it to the table, and one of them asks you if you used any animal products to bake it, like milk or eggs; they're both vegan. You tell them the truth, and one of them decides to have a slice anyway, just to avoid making you feel bad.

What happened in the end? Did they invite you on the trip? We shouldn't even talk about the result, because you now appreciate the different layers of complexity that were ignored in the process. Even if we agreed on the definition of success, namely getting invited to the trip, it unintentionally changed to simply baking a good cake at some point. Although I'm not saying this approach had no chance of success, you weren't maximizing the probabilities of achieving the success we agreed on.

Why was this a good time to start learning how to bake a cake? Why did you pick a foreign recipe? Why couldn't you check the ingredients before committing to choosing that recipe? But most importantly, why did you miss the conversations about the organic tea they liked? Why didn't you remember they were vegan if you all had dinner after class last week? The digital irreverent would've started by asking, 'Why should I bake a cake in the first place? Why is the trip important for me? What do the people that go on the trip have in common? What do they value? What are all the possible ways I can think of for having a chance to be invited? Is there any obvious one, like explaining why it's important for me and directly asking if I can join, or even offering my help with any preparation needed? Do I know of anybody who's been rejected before?

This is why *The Digital Irreverent Playbook* starts with redefining success or reconnecting with success. Sometimes, we don't even need to do real work to achieve the outcomes we want; however, we live in a world where most of the people are too busy baking cakes. The foreign recipe, the foreign ingredients, and acquiring a new skill are an analogy for ever-changing technologies and tools. The organic tea and the vegan friend are an analogy for how crucial it is to get to know our customers. The scenario of trying to bake the cake a second time reflects the idea of escalation of commitment. You didn't bake it the second time to maximize the chances of getting invited on the trip; you did it just to deliver a better cake and finish the task you set out to do.

This also represents the difference between achieving an output and achieving an outcome. The output is a result of the variables within the same system, whereas the outcome depends on variables *outside* the system. You can be perfect at everything and still not get invited on the trip; however, to maximize the chances of achieving that outcome, you should understand both the internal variables of your system and the external variables you don't control, such as your friend's dietary restrictions.

In the business world, we usually bake cakes in teams, and many believe that if each one delivers their part, we'll achieve overall success. However, as a digital irreverent, I believe the only way to maximize the chances of getting invited on the trip is by everybody understanding this as success and thinking beyond the cake. Even if you all agreed that baking the cake was the right way to maximize your chances of success, maybe somebody in the team would've realized that replacing milk and eggs with vegan alternatives would've avoided a painful outcome.

Sharing the same definition of success in a team, even if it maximizes the chances of success, doesn't necessarily make work easier. It requires a good understanding of the problem and an environment with a high level of safety and trust to effectively calibrate decision-making. We'll talk more about this in Chapter 5, when we delve into the sharing ownership topic.

WHAT IS SUCCESS?

Going back to the company objectives, how do companies define success? Simon Sinek, in his book *The Infinite Game,* proposes that ultimate success could be defined as follows: just keep playing the game. In the introduction, we discussed the difference in companies' lifespans between 1950s and 2010. Simon proposes that the business world is effectively an infinite game: there's no one winner, and the ultimate objective is to keep playing the game.

If you defined success as building a business that lasts 250 years, as a way of stating that you want to keep playing the business game for generations, it would be almost impossible to translate this objective into concrete actions, namely what the team should work on this year, this quarter, and this week. Because the human mind can't easily operate at that level of abstraction, attaining alignment in day-to-day decision-making would be almost impossible, considering individual interpretations of what's required to achieve that success. The outcomes needed to maximize the chances of achieving longevity also depend on the life stage of the company.

Let's consider different definitions of success with respect to the company stage. Although this isn't an exact science, I'll share my current understanding on the tradeoffs.

Early-stage startups have only two ways to keep playing the game in the next stage. One entails securing investment through angel investors, venture capital, or other corporates, and the other entails breaking even, which implies generating enough revenue to cover the costs of the business operation and thus generate profits. If you're trying to secure an investment with an angel investor at a very early stage, sometimes having a great story, proof of idea of what you want to build, some evidence of this being the right problem to solve, and the right solution can be enough. For this stage, securing an investment round could be a very solid definition of success; the event of securing the expected investment contains within it the combined criteria the market uses to measure the value of what you're building. Breaking even or extending your runway, which refers to how many months your company can live without additional investment, may also be an excellent definition of success at this early stage.

When you're over that stage and looking to secure higher investment, there are some patterns that the industry will expect you to meet. How fast is your user base growing? What's the cost of acquiring each customer? If you're generating revenue, how fast is that revenue growing? Have you achieved product market fit? Investors will have different variations on these questions depending on their strategy, regarding both industry and market conditions; however, they'll usually exhibit a converging pattern. In business categories that are exponentially growing their penetration, some investors will prefer to grab as much market share as possible, only later figuring out how to monetize the products.

After experiencing the exponential growth of Google, investors in Facebook knew the importance of network externalities early on; therefore, Microsoft decided to step in with $240 million before the Facebook executives had any solid monetization strategy. However, the social network had around 50 million active users and was riding on a very aggressive expansion trajectory. On the other hand, most business categories define success at this stage when the company reaches an initial user base that loves the product they build and are willing to pay for it. The initial challenge entails serving the first generation of customers in a way that compels them to engage with the product and come back for more. Before that point is reached, it's very difficult to scale. The next challenge entails being able to monetize this customer base at a much higher rate than it's costing you to acquire new customers. In other words, the Customer Acquisition Cost should be a fraction of the Customer's Lifetime Value. The Customer's Lifetime Value can be calculated as the Monthly Average Revenue per Customer multiplied by the average number of months a customer remains active. A good example of a definition of success in a SaaS product could be reaching a ratio of 3.5 between Customer Acquisition Cost and Lifetime Value.

In this scenario, a crucial caveat is that the main investors' internal definition of success is selling the shares of this company in the future at a much higher valuation. However, this is not something that will necessarily enable your company to live longer. It's just one of the rules of the game regarding when you should bring these types of investors on board.

Bigger companies also have a duty towards their shareholders; however, these shareholders are different from the early-stage investors. The company's market share, profit margins, and brand awareness play a much more crucial role. An example of a definition of success for a large, profitable company could be reaching a certain profit percentage as a direct result of their business operation. This is usually referred to as the Operating EBITDA.

An excellent example of someone challenging these definitions of success is displayed in the letters Jeff Bezos wrote to investors in the early days of Amazon. They were written in the initial stage of the internet, and despite the predominant investment culture at that time, Bezos clearly explained to his shareholders the importance of playing the long game. He consistently explained how big the company could grow, how big e-commerce was going to be in the future, and the immense opportunity they were presented with. However, to capitalize on that opportunity, he firmly believed they shouldn't focus on profit maximization at that stage.

If you feel there's something missing—that the long game can't be defined just by these types of KPIs—you're right. What's missing is something you can find in the book *Exponential Organizations* by Peter Diamandis. He shares the MTP (massive transformative purpose) idea, which poses the critical question: Why does the company exist in the first place? If the only objective was ensuring that the founders and the investors make a lot of money, that wouldn't be enough to explain our digital landscape.

To give you some MTP scenarios, Google had for many years said they existed to 'Organize the world's information.' Amazon wants to be the most customer-centric company in the world. SpaceX wants to make our species multiplanetary. You get the idea. So now playing the infinite game comes with a purpose, and an MTP is the spinal cord of that journey. By embracing this idea, you can even change the priority of the different definitions of success we discussed before. Your MTP could become your real definition of success, while the other definitions are just a way to extend your lifespan.

Therefore, you have bigger chances of fulfilling your MTP. This is effectively what drives you to play the long game.

UNDERSTANDING OBJECTIVES

How can these ideas be applied at any company?

Using these ideas, I believe there are three types of objectives you can set in a company.

1. **Objectives deriving directly from your massive transformative purpose.**

   How could you get closer to making our species multiplanetary if you're only selling plane tickets—even if that makes you profitable? The consistency in being able to connect with these purposes is a key element for playing the infinite game. People who paste Apple stickers in their cars don't do it because the company had amazing quarterly results; they do it because they're aligned with what they perceive the company believes, which feeds a virtuous cycle of loyalty, brand awareness, and growth. What is the KPI that represents your MTP the most? When Google bought YouTube in 2006, they had the ambition to make it bigger than TV; therefore, they chose to track the number of hours watched per day. They could have chosen to track active users, ads revenue, or other KPIs that responded more directly to the company-stage driven goals I just proposed; but without an objective linked to a higher definition of success, you'll fail at playing the infinite game. At Edenred UAE, we're passionate about financial inclusion, and even if we could be running a profitable business considering only financial KPIs, we chose to track and set objectives related to how we drive a cashless economy in the markets we operate.

2. **Time-bound objectives.**
   This refers to results that should happen within a certain timeframe to keep the organization in the game, and can be either financial or non-financial. Securing a series A investment round, the first round after the seed stage that can span between $1.5 million and $15 million, can be one of these objectives. If you don't do this in a certain time window, the company will probably die. Complying with certain regulations can also be a time-bound objective because it's time-sensitive, and you should do it to keep playing the game.

   Another example could be achieving a double-digit profit margin, which might be a condition to meet your shareholders' expectations. This second category of objectives, which is the most common one, is generally a contract between the organization and its stakeholders, such as investors, regulators, and partners. It can also be a contract within the organization. If you run a small family business where you're the owner, who'll hold you accountable for attaining a certain profitability in Q3? Maybe no one will; however, it might be productive for you to set up these types of goals and try to achieve a higher level of success.

   Besides the time sensitivity aspect, one common denominator of this type of objective is that you don't need to—and in fact, shouldn't—maximize them at all costs. For instance, it will be of no value securing a series A investment ten times larger than what you really need; it would also be a waste of time to comply with regulations that don't apply to you. Moreover, if you could press a button that could earn you a profit margin of three digits for the next quarter, I wouldn't bet on any publicly listed company CEO advocating for it if they don't know how to sustain this result over time. On the other hand, you're always incentivized to maximize the outcome of whatever's derived directly from your MTP. If, for instance, SpaceX is able to conduct missions to two or three separate planets without significantly increasing the risk of the company failing, why wouldn't they try it? If YouTube could improve its user flow and experience to the point where it can migrate all hours of TV watched to its own platform and content, why wouldn't they do it?. The catch is that the MTP-driven objectives are usually the most difficult, but they're more consistent over time.

3. **Enabling objectives.**
   This category of objectives is more related to how you do things to achieve sustainability. Exhibiting a low employee turnover, having a high cyber-security maturity in your team, or improving your application's performance by migrating to a new cloud provider won't be directly derived from your MTP, and these factors might not even be a condition for achieving this year's result; however, it's likely that by not focusing on them this year, next year's time-bound objectives could be jeopardized. Focusing on this category of objectives can crucially enable a company

to play the long game; the organization risks making very poor decisions if they optimize for only financial results over a short period of time. Enabling objectives are usually leading indicators of future financial results. For instance, you might have lost zero clients in a given year; however, if you observe a significant reduction in their satisfaction score, it's just a matter of time until the bucket starts leaking.

My recommendation for your irreverent journey is that you redefine success by combining these three types of objectives. With regard to the thing that derives directly from our massive transformative purpose, what should we do in this cycle? Which are the time-bound objectives—financial and non-financial—that we should meet in the same time window, and what are the enablers that should be on track for us to continue playing the game in the next cycle?

CONNECTION WITH THE OBJECTIVES

In my experience, I've seen teams connecting with their objectives at three different levels.

1. **Global connection**: This is when the person or team directly understands how what they're doing connects with the company's success. Their individual and team objectives can be easily linked and cascaded from the global objectives. You can see this level of connection

in high-performance sports teams, where there's an evident synchronicity and fluidity in the players' actions, and where each member understands the full context and reacts accordingly.

2. **Local connection**: The team and the team members understand the impact of their actions, and even measure it; however, they're not necessarily able to connect this to the company's global success. Although they know they're improving and evolving in baking flavorful vegan cakes, they don't relate to why they're baking cakes in the first place. What will the cakes be used for later? This is the most common level of connection within teams working at large companies.

3. **Authority connection**: This indicates that the team members are doing something they were requested to do, and that their success is in fulfilling their request without developing any connection with the outcomes or a deeper understanding of the purpose. This can be seen in some government entities across the world, where certain people have the authority to dictate rules or activities; however, the people who execute them don't really connect to why they've chosen that particular course of action in the first place. As you can imagine, a digital irreverent can't accept this last level. We should all be aiming to achieve the first level of connection, namely the global level.

In 2018, John Doerr launched a book titled *Measure What Matters*. Using principles he'd learned at Intel and successfully applied at Google, he explains the OKRs (Objectives and Key Results) concept. This is a hierarchical approach to goal-setting, where the objective is a high-level ambitious goal that's long-term in nature. The key results are specific KPI targets: when we meet them in a shorter term, we know we're on our way to achieving that objective.

One of the things I like the most about this approach is that the hierarchy it provides enables you to connect all levels of the organization to very clear KPIs and a common definition of success.

To provide an example, if we chose to use the time-bound objective of achieving X revenue by the end of the year, I could choose two key results that indicate we're on our way to achieving that goal. One is achieving X number of products sold, and the second is increasing our average sale price. These two key results can be matched to a quarterly target. A specific team can even have the number of products sold as an objective, and can define specific key results that enable them to improve that objective.

In the preceding scenario, one key result could be related to acquiring new customers in a certain region, and maybe another one could be related to improving their retention rate in a segment where they lost sales. This demonstrates a method of nesting objectives in a manner that enables them to remain dependent and that can be cascaded in a very clear way. Objectives and key results are being utilized by the best digital native companies worldwide—a method I strongly recommend for applying the definition of success at different levels.

ANSWER THESE QUESTIONS

1. How do you approach your own real definition of success? Take your time to understand what you're currently optimizing for.
2. Who benefits from this?
3. What are the incentives?
4. How can you replace this with the three types of objectives providing a balanced definition: the ones linked with a massive transformative purpose, the time-bound objectives, and the enabling objectives? Do you have a massive transformative purpose? Can you start with that?
5. How can you eliminate authority-based connections?
6. How can you attain a global level of connection with the right objectives for your company's stage?
7. How can you ensure you share common definitions of success across the team?
8. How can you apply objectives and key results to enable you to drive this change?

What are the conditions you need in a team to help you work this way? That's what I'll share with you in the next chapter.

CHAPTER 4

STEP 2:
STRUCTURE YOUR TEAM

Autonomous, interdisciplinary, and complete

There's an African proverb that says, 'If you want to go fast, go alone. If you want to go far, go together.' Now that you have clear tools to redefine or to reconnect with success, who do you want to have next to you? Better yet, who do you *need* to have next to you to maximize the chances of achieving that success? How do you build your team? The reason I liked that African proverb is because it resonates with the infinite game idea. Why would you need to go fast if you're not optimizing for longevity? At least in the business world, this long-term perspective is essential. We can easily remember names of famous founders, CEOs, and successful individuals who achieved great things; however, we should also remember that they never achieved these things alone.

In this chapter, I'll assume you're not working alone, or at least, that you're not planning to work alone for long. *Setting up teams* isn't something that appeared in the Digital Age. It's almost embedded in our DNA: humans have been organizing in groups for ages. However, we should determine how we can identify the right way of setting up a team with big chances of succeeding in a Digital Age.

In other words, how do you set up your irreverent team? I'll then walk you through some questions and ideas about how to solve this puzzle yourself and maximize the chances of achieving the success you learned to define in the previous chapter. But before that, let me share some ideas that will help you understand the tradeoffs around the decisions related to building a team.

CONWAY'S LAW

In 1967, the American computer scientist Melvin Conway shared his understanding of how an organizational structure shaped the systems that the same organization builds. He stated, 'Any organization that designs a system produces a design whose structure mirrors the organization's communication structure.' Conway's Law simply means that the way you structure and organize your team can greatly impact the architecture of the product that you build. We now understand the importance of being adaptable and of being able to react effectively to customer needs: these abilities can continuously drive impact. What team structure optimizes for adaptability? What are the attributes of a team that truly engages with the customer's needs?

Let me reuse the cake analogy to illustrate how we can shape scenarios of different teams with the same goal, and what each of them ends up optimizing for. Let's assume your goal is still getting invited to the yoga retreat, and that you have three friends who are committed to helping you achieve this goal.

First, there's Scenario One: You assign one of your friends the task of buying the best-quality almond flour; you assign your second friend the task of buying the ripe bananas, fresh milk, and eggs; and you assign your third friend the task of baking the cake. In this scenario, you're responsible for choosing the recipe and explaining the steps to each one of them.

Now, let's consider Scenario Two: The four of you are responsible for choosing the recipe, and once you're aligned, you distribute the assignments in the following way: Two of your friends will do the shopping for the ingredients of the recipe you chose together, and the other friend will do the baking with you. However, you'll be more focused on the service and preparation of the tea. The two friends that did the shopping have autonomy in deciding who buys what and where.

Finally, let's imagine Scenario Three: Two of your friends are responsible for understanding the preferences of your yoga colleagues and their expectations about the retreat. Your remaining friend and you will be focused on whatever's needed regarding food and service, but you and your two researcher friends will decide what's really going to 'move the needle' and how you get invited to the trip.

Which team scenario has the highest chances of getting you invited to the yoga retreat?

Depending on the assumptions you make, any scenario can be the best. What could make the first scenario win? The first assumption you should make for that scenario to win is explained as follows: To get invited to the yoga trip, you should have your friends over and surprise them with a cake you baked. The second assumption is that the right cake to bake is the banana cake with the ingredients that were already presented in the recipe. You're probably ensuring that your friends will specialize in what they need. You'll get the best-quality flour. You'll get the ripe bananas, fresh milk, and eggs, and ensure that someone's dedicated to baking the cake. All these actions are aimed at creating the conditions for baking the best banana cake that your yoga classmates have ever eaten, and if there are other new joiners who also try to impress them with a banana cake, you'll be better than them because you'll be specializing in the best-quality ingredients and the best baking process.

The assumptions for the second scenario to be successful are as follows: First, you should still bake a cake to get invited to the retreat; however, in this case, it's not obvious which cake you should bake to impress them. The second assumption gives you flexibility in who buys what and where. Maybe you and your friends already have relevant experience baking a specific type of cake that's not banana cake. You even have the chance to decide what cake to bake depending on the time you have and the available ingredients. While you might be successful with this scenario, you and your friends may never become the best banana cake bakers.

By contrast, the third scenario implies a minimal assumption, which is necessary for success. Basically, it assumes that you haven't completely figured out how to get invited on the trip and that you should find a way to achieve this success. Although dedicating effort and time to understanding the problem will move you farther away from becoming the best banana cake baker, it'll also give you the highest chances of success when you don't have that clarity initially.

Most Product teams get hired to bake cakes, even if this doesn't always mean optimizing for the company's success. The industrial-minded organizations have taught us that sometimes we don't achieve the success we defined because our friend in the first scenario didn't buy the right flour, or because our baker friend took longer than expected; however, we always rely on the assumption that the decision about what to do isn't questionable. Generally, the decision about what to do is separated from the people who effectively do the work. If we use Conway's Law to understand this scenario, we can say that most teams are designing products with a high level of technical specialization and a false sense of certainty about what should be built.

I like to categorize the ways of organizing teams into three types. The first is the **technical function–driven method**. That would essentially entail scaling the first scenario and having a team of people specializing in almond flour and reporting to a person who used to be an almond flour purchaser themselves. This is an effective approach when the success of the organization is reliant on dominating the complexity of a specific technical function. You can easily find these examples in academia or in the consultancy world.

The second is the **product- or system-driven method**, which entails having different people working in the cake team as a means of learning and developing different techniques of baking cakes. They'll know what a great cake tastes like, and they'll even be able to get feedback about the cake and improve the processes. In that team, you may have bakers, flour specialists, and a person who does general shopping; however, you might miss a certain level of specialization that you had in the technical function–driven teams.

The third type of team follows the **outcome- or result-driven method**. This is usually the case where you have a certain timeframe to achieve an objective; you should combine different technical functions and even different products and systems to achieve this. If you need to get invited to that yoga retreat in two weeks but you don't have clarity on how to achieve it, the third type of team is probably what you need.

Most companies in the world during the early decades of the Digital Age default to technical function–driven teams. Sales, marketing, engineering, and design are structured as separate departments. Maybe there's also some interdisciplinary manner of organizing these departments, such as a project-based categorization, or some agile approach to product development; however, they still identify more with their technical expertise than with the problem they're solving. This is why, when you meet people outside of the work environment and ask them what they do for a living, you're more likely to hear things such as 'Software Engineer at Company X' or 'Marketing Analyst at Company Y' than something such as 'Improve the conversion of the e-commerce funnel at Company Z'. That's effectively what we learned from industrial-minded companies, where the Engineer reports to the Engineering Manager, the Sales Executive reports to the Sales Manager, the Marketing Analysts report to the Marketing Manager, and so on.

These technical function–driven organization charts as well as the predominant school systems are designed to make us effective at one specific thing, and somebody else will 'require' from us what they need around the ability we developed.

In the Digital Age, that asymmetry between the person dictating what we should do and the person executing that action no longer makes sense. Most product development decisions are context-dependent and have many variables that should be carefully managed. In this space, there are multiple possible solutions for every problem, and for every solution, there are many methods of implementation. Designers and builders should make assumptions for every detail that's not defined about a solution. The irreverent team doesn't waste time pretending they can go after every definition needed; they simply get involved with the understanding of the initial problem and its context, thereby improving and aligning their assumptions.

Having explained all this, what type of organization structure should you choose for your team? The answer is all of them.

Depending on the stage and size of your team, there's a healthy way of combining them all. In a preceding section, I explained that the outcome-driven team is ideal for uncertain scenarios; however, you can't work for long on an endeavor if everything around you is uncertain. At some point, you defined a product; at another, you defined the technology you'll be basing that product on; at another, you choose a target customer, and so on. If for some reason your banana cake approach to the yoga retreat problem was successful, maybe you decide to open a vegan bakery next to the yoga studio. In that case, there might be nothing wrong with having a product-based team that takes care of baking cakes from start to end.

That's because you're way beyond the point of asking yourself if you need a cake or not. You should just scale how many cakes you can bake that are good enough to be sold. If you keep scaling, and at some point the almond flour (which was so difficult to find when you baked your first banana cake) becomes a key ingredient of your most successful cakes, you might even want to start producing that internally and have part of your team specialize in almond flour. That could be the case for a technical function–driven team.

To share an example of a real case in the digital world, when I was working at Mercado Libre, most of the teams were product-based. For instance, we had a Search product team and a Checkout product team. At the same time, we needed to have some technical function–driven teams with a deep level of specialization, like Architecture and Networking, that were contributing to all of the products at the same layer.

Meanwhile, we had some quarters where we needed teams to do specific missions such as migrations, assessing a new M&A, and rolling out changes that affected several products. These were good examples of outcome-based teams, which after achieving or maybe failing at the desired outcome moved on to a new mission, or simply went back to a product-driven team. The dominance of the product-based approach can be explained as follows: Although the complexity wasn't significant in the technical layer we utilized for building the applications, it was in the interdisciplinary nature of the problems we needed to solve to drive impact in the business and improve these products in a scalable way.

For instance, if the biggest opportunity to contribute to your success is reducing the dropout in the checkout flow of your e-commerce platform, this might be achieved by a combination of completely different efforts, such as reducing the screen loading time in the app through technical optimizations, improving the user experience by using a cleaner design, or negotiating the shipping costs with your provider to reduce the corresponding fee for your buyers when they're making the decision to pay.

The product-based team should be obsessed with measuring their product and how their users behave around it, which enables them to combine unrelated solutions to drive the desired impact in a converging manner. If the same challenge was presented to a technical-driven team receiving requirements from someone else, it would be in the best case much slower in identifying and attempting improvements that depend on connecting layers. In contrast, after the introduction of Infrastructure as a Service and Platform as a Service solutions by Cloud providers, the product- or system-driven teams became more empowered as they started having a commoditized infrastructure layer instead of having to rely on a specialized team across the organization.

INVERSE CONWAY'S LAW

With this evolution, teams started scaling in a different way. They owned their own infrastructure, and were communicating with each other through APIs (Application Programming Interfaces). This is a technology-agnostic form of communication between two systems or two different parts of the same system. The technology being used to develop System A versus the one being used to develop System B isn't a concern if the contract represented by the API is the same for both systems. Using this approach, teams can have a high level of autonomy and empowerment; they could operate as if they were different companies on a small scale.

This approach will result in a specific type of team by applying the inverse case of Conway's Law: Once you know how your system design should look, you can shape a team around that objective.

This is exactly what companies like Amazon did when they started scaling. Small teams could run simultaneous experiments without depending on each other and using the same connecting systems. Business decisions are taken locally at the team level because work is designed to make it very cheap to fail: the company exposes experiments to small, controlled audiences and makes it seamless to release and roll back these experiments. (When I say 'team level', I mean a group of not more than eight people.) One of Jeff Bezos' famous laws about teams is the two-pizza team law, which states that a team shouldn't be larger than the number of people that can be fed with two pizzas.

ENGINEERING CULTURE

One of the most famous models of small interdisciplinary teams that are loosely coupled and connect with each other through APIs is Spotify, whose Engineering team released a series of videos explaining their working culture—a culture that was highly influenced by the Agile Manifesto, by some practices from Scrum, and perhaps also by Extreme Programming and other principles and methodologies that will be discussed in Chapter 6.

Defining your objectives and the key results aligned with your success using the tools described in the previous chapter will be the starting point for building your irreverent team.

However, I don't mean that you should be able to cascade the OKRs right away before assembling your team. By doing that, you'll be creating two problems.

1. You'll be directly creating a result-driven team without considering your other options. This team will achieve a result, but won't necessarily take enough time to dive deeply into a product or its technical layers as a method of growing its impact over time. Depending on the time window you're optimizing for, you might prefer to first analyze the tradeoffs between this type of team, or instead have a technical function–driven or product-driven team.
2. You'll be depriving your team of the responsibility of defining their own OKRs, a point we'll discuss in the next chapter.

I propose the following: First, define the key battles that should be addressed to achieve the main objective. I call them battles because they're not trivial. Although they imply an effort, a decision, and a challenge, they might not be easy to express as OKRs immediately. If you're in the situation of trying to get invited to the yoga retreat with the help of your three friends, your number one battle would be understanding your classmates' preferences and what quick actions you could take to increase your chances of getting invited to the trip. No other key battle is important until that one is tackled; however, what happens when you reach a larger scale? Let's suppose you have a bakery next to the yoga studio with a massive transformative purpose of becoming the preferred bakery for the yogi community, and assume you have an objective of achieving $250,000 in revenue within the year.

Examples of battles could be (1) mastering the sourcing of the ingredients, (2) perfecting the baking processes, and (3) scaling sales efficiently.

With these three battles, it could be reasonable to assume that if I excel in the three of them, I'll have good chances of positively impacting the revenue. In these examples, each battle has a strong common denominator related to the technical function or process. The irreverent leader will try to minimize the number of key battles presented at a time. When many things are important, nothing is critical; however, the emphasis is still on having reasonably small teams. In other words, if I ignore the two-pizza team recommendation from Jeff, I'll also be increasing the risk of having a difficult decision-making process.

What would happen if I wanted to unify the three examples in one team with a key battle that's only about revenue?

Then I'll probably be missing the advantage of specialization in sub-systems, and would also be creating inefficiency. How critical is the salesperson's participation in sourcing the right ingredients for the cake? How important is the baker's contribution to improving the sales pitch? There's no right or wrong answer, but if the natural contribution between these three battles isn't clear, it would make sense to have different people dedicated to each one of them. This doesn't mean they shouldn't communicate or align, but they'll be mainly focusing on one battle at a time. Moreover, these battles aren't expected to represent 100% of the team effort. I believe 70 to 80% of the effort is more than enough, and the teams will autonomously decide how they'll divide the 20 or 30% of the remaining effort.

In the cake shop scenario and in most businesses, there are three possible approaches for a product- or system-driven team.

One would be to consider your key business processes as products or systems: this means that your ingredients supply, baking, and selling could be optimized independently. For instance, your ingredients supply can become so efficient and of such good quality that you can start supplying other smaller bakeries with the same team. When Amazon spun off Fulfilment By Amazon and Amazon Web Services as independent businesses, it became a case of having optimized these internal systems with such a level of autonomy up to a point where it made sense to make them separate businesses.

The second possible approach is doing this by product or product line, which would be like having a team dedicated to cakes and another dedicated to bread; each team will own the whole process for its own product, from sourcing ingredients to selling. In this example, this approach doesn't seem very reasonable because we might not perceive a clear gain in specializing the sourcing and the sales system; but if we work with a product or in an industry where these processes don't share a significant common denominator between products, it might make more sense.

The third possible approach is the combination of the previous two: you have specialized processes per product line. You can often find this in large companies where products are departmentalized.

TAKE ACTION

What are the top three battles you should tackle to achieve your main objective?

What's the common denominator in each one of them? Is it about a product? A technology? A process?

Where does the complexity reside in each case? Is there a technical complexity? Is it about understanding customer needs? Is it about complex organization and alignment?

I recommend identifying your key battles by focusing on your objective and trying to identify the layers that should be moved for this objective to happen. What KPIs should be improved for the objective to be achieved?

Once you define your team, its members will be able to define the key results for those objectives much more easily, based on the way you chose the key battle. What is your minimum viable team for each key battle you chose? Can you afford to have only one person that knows how to bake in your bakery? What is the minimum redundancy you need in different positions? What are the synergies when you have more than one person sharing the same technical specialization?

EXTREME TEAMS

In 1999, Kent Beck, a project leader working at Chrysler, wrote a book titled *Extreme Programming*. The idea entailed presenting a software development methodology that could optimize for frequent releases, high quality, and quick adaptation to a changing environment. The minimum viable team in this extreme programming approach comprises two Software Engineers; because the methodology provides the Engineers with the ability to review each other's code and make decisions quickly, it's very powerful. Most of the leading native digital companies apply this methodology at some level. So, when I build my own teams, I try to consider that many technical positions work effectively in pairs, and that these pairs can also be embedded within an interdisciplinary team.

An example of a Digital Product Development team I set up is composed by two back-end Software Engineers, two Mobile Software Engineers, one Product Designer, and one Product Manager.

Why do Software Engineers come in pairs, contrary to the rest of the team members?

Here, I'm applying XP (Extreme Programming) and assuming that a Software Engineer could also contribute to reviewing the design of a Product Designer and the discovery work of a Product Manager; however, it's very difficult for a Product Manager or Product Designer to review an Engineer's code if they don't have the minimum technical knowledge. You might wonder, 'What do you mean by saying a Software Engineer can review the work of a Product

Manager?' Well, this is an irreverent team, and all Software Engineers in an irreverent team understand product; we'll discuss this idea in the next chapter.

Variations of this team might have fewer Engineers; however, to ensure they have the ability to practice XP across different layers or technology stacks, we might also introduce an XP equivalent for design or product management.

Another feature of my irreverent teams is that there's absolutely no position dedicated only to following processes. For instance, I never hired a Project Manager. This doesn't mean that nobody in the team can do project management work. That's absolutely expected in many scenarios; however, playing that role is different from having a position that does *only* that. In my irreverent teams, every position (at its core) is based on the ability to build something and solve a problem; positions aren't formed to follow a process that somebody outside of the team defined.

I also avoid having dedicated people for Quality Assurance: this usually promotes the wrong habits in Software Engineers, and we already have enough tools and knowledge to automate a big portion of the required QA. We have practices for minimizing impact when things go wrong, and, if for some reason, it makes sense to do some manual testing, what's the shame in having the same people in the team dedicating one or two hours every once in a while to dive deeper into their own product? For special occasions, you can also outsource this work.

What makes the talent in your team good irreverent talent?

I'd like to frame this question while considering two dimensions.

The first dimension is learning agility. This refers to how you figure out what to do when you don't know what to do. How quickly can you adapt to different circumstances, scenarios, and problems? Are you curious about what you don't understand?

The second dimension is agency. That refers to how empowered you feel in being able to solve things regardless of your position, the limitations of your budget, or anything around you. People with a low sense of agency expect things to be defined for them. By contrast, people with a high sense of agency know that if there's a will, there's a way. They feel accountable and responsible for making things happen. Of course, this should not be confused with the lonely hero nobody wants to have in their team; that individual should be resourceful and a great team player.

What's the role of a leader in this context? Honestly, in my ideal irreverent team, I don't need a predefined leader. Having people with a high sense of agency and great learning agility should be enough to tackle great challenges. In reality, it's very rare to find a team like this because of the industrial-minded inheritance I explained before. In most of the teams I built, I've always tried to have one leader from Design, Engineering, or Product Management that could mentor the team in organization and decision-making. Why is one leader enough? Depending on the seniority of each person in the team and of this leader, this person has enough experience solving problems similar to what the team is facing, but has access to other leaders and experts; therefore, he can get help when needed.

In the example of Spotify's engineering culture, they introduced the idea of chapters, where people of the same technical discipline across different teams have collaboration and alignment spaces aimed at evolving their solutions and knowledge, which also induces consistency in the execution of that layer across the company. I usually apply this as well.

THE IRREVERENT LEADER

In most scenarios, the irreverent leader ends up doing three things:

1. Helping the team connect the massive transformative purpose of the organization with the objectives in the different working cycles,
2. Helping unblock dependencies between internal and external teams, and
3. Managing talent to ensure the right people are sitting at the right place and the right feedback loops are happening.

The irreverent leader is also effective at promoting inclusion consciousness. Diversity is a reality with infinite dimensions. Inclusion is a conscious choice that enables people to identify these dimensions in the people around us and bring them together with the same opportunities as everyone else.

A team with this consciousness will be more effective at detecting problem-solving patterns and understanding the reality around them.

KEY TAKEAWAYS

To build your irreverent team, the following steps are crucial.

1. Define the key battles related to your main objective.
2. Set up empowered product-driven teams responsible for each key battle.
3. Technical function–driven teams should enable the creation of a product (or products) carrying a high technical complexity in at least one of its parts, or in one of its growth stages.
4. Outcome-driven teams will be, apart from the founding team that built the first POC or MVP of the business, an on-demand need once the product structure is defined.
5. Remember the two-pizza team size and drive technical work in pairs, based on XP, to leverage agility.
6. Don't hire people responsible only for processes; everyone should be able to participate in building or effectively solving a problem.
7. Hire prioritizing learning agility and agency.

8. Teams don't always need a dedicated leader, but the closest leader should help them connect the objectives with the overall success, unblock dependencies, and ensure they have the right talent.

Now, what conditions should you put in place for this irreverent team to drive the impact you need?

CHAPTER 5

STEP 3:
SHARE OWNERSHIP

Challenge the illusion of efficiency

After redefining success and setting up your team, what's the main condition that distinguishes it as an irreverent team? The condition is that each team member should have a clear share of ownership of the business' success. That's why the focus of this chapter and the third step of the *Digital Irreverent Playbook* is learning how to share ownership.

As you'd probably expect, I'll revisit the reason most teams don't share ownership nowadays, and what I mean by share ownership. Regarding the illusion of control, the industrial mindset believes that to achieve a specific output, you should optimize the different inputs. If each person in the team is owning and executing the right tasks, the output will be delivered, and success will be achieved.

However, we proved that in the digital space, there are many more variables than the inputs, and success doesn't depend on outputs, but on outcomes, which have external components that we don't control. In a supply-driven economy, we could pursue efficiency by improving processes for a commoditized workforce, thus achieving more optimal results. Although I'm sure that responsibility and effort are rewarded in this context, it's not expected to have team members questioning the process or proposing new ways of doing things based on the probability of achieving a better outcome. This type of behavior would stress the industrial-minded management (which understands how expensive any mistake could be) and might jeopardize the security of their job or their position at the company, which was probably obtained through many years of effort and loyalty. That's the key point: A high level of ownership doesn't optimize for safety. It's no coincidence that Maslow's Hierarchy of Needs is effectively a pyramid where safety is at the base, and that the higher you go, the fewer people you'll find actively pursuing a higher level of needs related to purpose and self-realization. Most people are still trying to optimize for physical or emotional safety; it's no wonder irreverent teams are hard to find, and successful native digital companies strive to generate psychologically safe environments where mistakes aren't punished and are even sometimes rewarded. The irony of the Digital Age, as can be observed in companies' lifespan reduction, is that the highest risk is *not* to take risks and trying to be safe at all costs doesn't guarantee safety.

In Chapter 3, I described the three levels of connections with goals. The first was the global level, the second was the local level, and the third was the authority level of connection. Sharing ownership means that you at least have a local level of connection and that every individual's partially or totally accountable for the result regardless of the role they play in the team. This accountability comes hand-in-hand with the empowerment, tools, and space to be part of the decision-making.

SHARING OWNERSHIP IS CRUCIAL IN THIS ENVIRONMENT

In this demand-driven economy, we almost never know beforehand which is the right problem to focus on, which is the right solution, and which is the best way to implement this solution; the only way to be effective and adapt quickly is to be close enough to the problems. That means having a team that's empowered to understand the context, define the problem, find the solutions, and make decisions with a high level of autonomy, which enables them to learn quickly from the environment and try again.

The real challenge, however, is not that most of the people that build digital products are working in a purely industrial manner and should adopt a digital working style, but that most of the teams that believe they're doing things in an agile digital way are actually inheriting and applying very strong components of the industrial mindset.

Anyone who's applying the scrum methodology by the book and having scrum masters facilitating the meetings, Product Owners defining the user stories, Software Engineers writing code, and Quality Assurance Engineers testing the applications, regardless of how often they review their backlog, is exhibiting a more industrial behavior—not a digital one.

The preceding scenario resembles a software factory. There's no shame in being a factory, especially if your success is primarily shipping code, and if your business relies on being paid for the applications delivered, regardless of the results it generates for your client's business.

On the other hand, if your success depends on the product you build being used and the impact it generates, if you rigidly apply these types of methodologies, you'll be assuming a much higher risk than most people think. In the scrum-by-the-book example, the Software Engineer probably doesn't have to fully own the quality. There's a Quality Assurance Engineer for that. The Engineer doesn't have to understand the problem behind the solution being implemented, because the user stories are supposed to be clearly pre-written by the Product Owner.

The Product Owner probably relies on higher-level requirements shared by stakeholders they call 'the business'. The scrum master is primarily responsible for facilitating meetings, and management is relieved because they implemented Scrum successfully. This team will mostly be safe as long as the business survives, and there will always be somebody to blame if things don't turn out as expected in the short term.

If I had the chance to meet this team and I asked the Software Engineer why he's developing user stories and how they're connected to the company goals, what are the chances of this person effectively understanding their real connection versus justifying that this was defined by the Product Owner (or any authority)? If I asked the Product Owner about the possible tradeoffs of the technical solution applied, would this person know the answer? When digital companies work with teams where responsibilities are completely segregated, many of the developed products never 'see the light of day' or require so many changes to make them work that a higher investment is needed. This is because they end up diverging from the hypotheses and needs assumed when the investment was decided.

THE LADDER OF OWNERSHIPS

Irreverent teams members have a high sense of ownership; because they see the team's success and the business's success as their responsibility, their decisions are aimed at creating a positive impact in the results, way beyond the tasks assigned. They dedicate effort to developing strong interpersonal collaboration, and their skills transcend what each team member initially specialized in. Therefore, they can successfully navigate the grey areas. This is more difficult than just trying to be safe, but a high-performing irreverent team is unstoppable because it succeeds at making complex problems simple through a common understanding of the problems and effective collaboration.

As Steve Jobs once said, 'Simple can be harder and complex. You have to work hard to get your thinking clean to make it simple.'

What should you do to drive this ownership? I'll share six steps for achieving this based on principles that worked for me in the past.

First, eliminate internal contracts.

Second, define your problem space and understand it.

Third, treat adults like adults.

Fourth, don't just trust. Verify.

Fifth, overcome the fancy office bias.

Sixth, reward success.

Now, let's discuss each one of them in more detail.

First, get rid of internal contracts. Whether implicit or explicit, internal contracts make you average. This is because they usually require an effort to clearly define the minimum acceptable terms, ignoring the endless possibilities of finding out the best solutions through engagement and collaboration. The Product Owner writing a story for the Software Engineer to develop is an implicit contract. What happens if the Software Engineer does more things than the story requested? What if by doing this, she or he even makes a mistake? If the Software Engineer and the Product Owner aren't prepared to have a discussion of what's the best solution to a given problem, the fact that one of them writes user stories doesn't make it better. I have nothing against somebody writing user stories. The problem is when that becomes the job of only one role in the team.

What I don't accept is that this document means more than the real understanding of the right solution for the right problem by everybody involved. In the last chapter, I mentioned that I have Product Managers, but not Product Owners, in my teams because one of the contracts we should break internally is calling one person an 'owner'. This is implicitly saying that everyone else is not.

Another example of internal contracts are SLAs (service level agreements). These are probably explicit contracts. For example, how long do you take to fix a high-priority bug? What is the longest a user would have to wait to get a response when there's an incident? The SLAs define a commitment of what will be the worst acceptable response time. In a team where everyone has a high sense of ownership, team members shouldn't adopt a very conservative time window to avoid blame; they should always do their best because they have skin in the game. Other teams will jump in to help them, because not solving that problem quickly enough will affect everyone's results. Moreover, a team member will have the understanding and the empowerment to question the real priority of the case being raised. This point doesn't mean that you'll be able to get rid of *all* SLAs on external contracts. For now, we can't assume that all the teams around you will be as irreverent as ours.

The second step is **defining your problem space and understanding it**. The global objectives of almost any digital endeavor are usually very far from clear instructions of how to build something. As we've seen in Chapter 3, they look more like business objectives that may change depending on the stage of the company and its context; the cascading of these objectives into local goals doesn't make it easier. We can't achieve these objectives if we don't understand the problems we should face to generate the outcomes driving these results, and we can't develop the right solutions either if we don't define these problems correctly. I believe that for every problem, there are infinite technical solutions and that choosing the right technical solution is highly dependent on optimally understanding this problem.

I consider it a huge risk to delegate this responsibility to only one role in the team. I think it's completely reasonable that one role in a team goes deeper into problem discovery; the problem space should be separated from the solution space, and the team should understand how the connection of both factors is everyone's responsibility. The previous chapters have revealed that baking a banana cake can never be the best solution if I don't understand how I can maximize the chances of getting invited to the Yoga retreat. You define the problem space by openly stating the gap between your main objective and your current scenario, and by inviting the team to state their hypotheses about how that gap can be closed and what opportunities could be identified. Although some team members can provide great value with experience in user research, data analytics, and product management, these skills should be used to simplify the problem space discussions with everyone involved and not as a way of simply segregating tasks between people.

The third step is to **treat adults like adults**. Sometimes, we believe that the more we digest the problem, analyze it, and specify the right solution, the more we simplify the work of our colleague who'll be executing that solution; thus, we believe we'll be able to move faster. Somebody doesn't get invited to the meeting to avoid wasting her or his time when important decisions are made there, and this person loses the context later. It's completely reasonable to think that most people would like to have a well-documented representation of whatever's expected from them, and that they need a simplified explanation of their roles. Although this can generate a sense of safety and clarity, we already know that this sense of certainty being transmitted is imagined and not real. For the team to be able to cope with the actual level of uncertainty, somebody always pays with effort at some point. A cascade of commitment is created where some people do the work several times and the pressure around deadlines and conditions to be met accumulates over time.

How do you work with people who expect everything to be digested for them? The first part of the answer is: You don't. You're not forced to invest in people that don't have the right level of agency or learning agility. If the person in your team doesn't engage with the idea of finding out ways of solving a problem or doesn't own a point of view that contributes to the scenario, that person is probably not right for your irreverent team.

The second part of the answer is that you should always take the first step at attempting to treat people like adults. Take your time to present the problems as they are, provide evidence, and facilitate the space for people to ask questions and give their opinion. Promote discussions based on evidence and data, take the time to check if your team understands the problems presented, and don't give weight to opinions only based on the level of seniority or the role in the team.

If you do all this, it's also important that you don't accept when somebody justifies that they don't understand something because it's not part of their job. One common symptom of not treating everyone as adults and having a more paternalistic approach is identifying when communication channels are restricted. Some people in the company are not allowed to talk to Software Engineers if they don't align first with Product Owners or Product Managers. Product Designers and Software Engineers can't align in a solution if the Product Manager isn't present (and other possible rules of this kind).

When you treat your team members like adults, you shouldn't tell them who they can speak to or not, and your default behavior will be trusting that they'll have the right criteria to manage this themselves, even if this effectively means redirecting the concern to another team member. However, this shouldn't happen because of a policy or rule, but because the person actually understands that this is the best way of solving the problem, which promotes more contextual decision-making and a better ability to adapt.

The fourth step is **don't just trust, verify**. This title, inspired by a famous quote in the crypo domain—'Don't trust. Verify.'—was in turn derived from a Russian proverb which can be interpreted as follows: If you want something done right, do it yourself. In the world of crypto, this means you shouldn't just trust. You can verify things by yourself because the blockchain is public, as opposed to centralized financial institutions which assume you should trust them about what's actually happening with your funds. The application of this idea in the behavior of an irreverent team is not that you shouldn't trust anyone. Its implication has more to do with having a common language and tools that anyone can use to verify that we're deciding or doing the most important thing we should be doing. This common language is established by a combination of goals, objectives, key results, KPIs, and even a clear definition of a problem space of what any irreverent team should have a common understanding of.

Let me illustrate this case by using an example from the yoga retreats problem. If I go to my team of friends responsible for baking and suddenly ask them to bake an apple pie instead of a banana cake, the conventional team will immediately start thinking about how to bake the best apple pie; they'll assume that because I'm the one trying to get invited on the trip, I know exactly what I need.

But an irreverent team would first verify the connection between the problem space and the solution space before they proceed. Assuming they already know that the purpose, namely to get invited to the yoga retreat, the first thing they'll do is ask me: Why do I think that an apple pie will increase the chances of getting invited on the trip, as opposed to the banana cake? There will be a lot of ingredients and time wasted if we make that change, so good luck convincing an irreverent team if you don't have good evidence of why they should change this.

Let's suppose you have a good reason to bake an apple pie instead of a banana cake. For instance, assume the almond flour you needed for the banana cake exceeds your budget. In that scenario, your irreverent team will ask you questions until they get to the real reason for the change: It's a budgetary matter. So, instead of starting to bake the apple pie, they'll choose to reframe the problem space. That's what maximizes the chances of being invited to the trip with this budget limit. Maybe someone has an idea of an alternative banana cake that costs less. Maybe the best decision is even going back to the drawing board to see if you should bake something to start with. It may also be the case that your calculation was wrong and somebody in the team proves that the banana cake can be perfectly baked without exceeding the budget.

The idea of 'Don't just trust, verify' is never about trusting the person or the intentions. It's about acknowledging that because we all have our biases and we all make mistakes, we should utilize the power of collective intelligence. Usually when I present this idea, it's interpreted as claiming that everyone should know about everything at the highest possible level, but that's not the point. We'll share ownership of the collective goals, and it's even recommended that some activities be performed by more than one role in the team. However, we don't have the same responsibilities.

I frame this idea as follows: There are still some things that a certain role can't fail at. My favorite analogy for explaining this point is the chess puzzle. If you like chess, you've probably seen chess puzzles in newspapers, magazines, or books, where a chessboard is presented in an advanced state of the game. Next to the image of the board, it says something like 'White to move and performs a checkmate in three'. That means there's a combination of moves that can get white to perform a checkmate in three moves. Let's suppose you're looking at this chess problem with your friend, who's a chess master, and you're not very experienced in chess, but at least know the rules. Your friend will certainly be able to solve the problem better than you, or at least faster than you; however, the fact that you at least know the rules of the game gives you enough power to be able to verify that his solution is correct, and this is exactly the point I want to make.

You want to have an irreverent team full of masters, but you don't want them being masters of the same thing. Everyone should know the rules of the game well enough to verify whether the decision-making is satisfactory. This is not only reflected in the invitation to question the Product Manager regarding the right definition of the problem space, but it also works in all directions. What's the evidence that the team should see to verify that the solution which the Software Engineer was executing was well-implemented? How can the team verify that the experience created by the Product Designer works? In every case, the answer is the same. We should proactively measure business KPIs, technical KPIs, and user experience KPIs in a way that ensures our hypothesis can be verified afterwards. We'll talk more about how to validate these hypotheses in Chapter 7, which is dedicated to embracing uncertainty.

Step 5 entails **overcoming the fancy office bias**. In 2009, two years after its IPO, Mercado Libre inaugurated new offices for its team in Buenos Aires. We moved from a normal office space in a very nice building to a specially designed space in one of the newest buildings in the city. It looked more like Silicon Valley compared with any other company office in Argentina at that time. It was the upgrade in our working environment that triggered a sense of engagement and belonging; however, I saw one person who didn't look that excited. That was Dani, our CTO, who explained his reasoning about the risk of having a fancy space as follows. To some people, the new space gave the feeling that all things were already taken care of as opposed to the feeling in the early years in the garage: back then, it was evident that there was no other way but to share the ownership of almost everything across the team. This point stuck with me throughout my career.

This idea of the fancy office bias is actually a close cousin to the Broken Window Theory introduced in 1984 by social scientists James Wilson and George Kelling who stated that visible signs of crime, anti-social behavior, and civil disorder create an urban environment that encourages further crime and disorder. This idea stated that policing methods that target minor crimes as vandalism, loitering, public drinking, and fare evasion promote unlawfulness, and that this was exactly the policy chosen by Rudy Giuliani in 1993 as an attempt to reduce crime in New York City when he was the mayor. Even if I can't confirm that the application of this policy was the reason crime reduced in New York City, I believe there's a lot of insight in this theory when we talk about sharing ownership.

When I joined Edenred in 2022, my team was far from irreverent and was exhibiting a behavior that tested my patience; the behavior had nothing to do with digital product development. Every time people left a meeting room, the chairs were left in disarray. The office assistant entered the room every time a meeting ended so he could put the chairs back in order. If I attend a meeting and I don't put at least my own chair back in order because I think somebody else will do it later or because I don't even see it as something to be done, how am I supposed to have a higher sense of ownership about the rest of the work I do at the company?

In 2023, I facilitated a training for my team where I couldn't wait to illustrate the example of the chair scenario so I could make a point about the importance of sharing ownership. At that point, we'd all gone through the real definition of success and setting up the teams; therefore, I asked the question, 'What would happen if our new definition of success would be achieving a high score in clients', partners', and employees' satisfaction about the conditions in which they find our meeting rooms?' Our office assistant was doing a great job, but what would happen when we scaled the number of clients, partners, employees, and meeting rooms we should serve? The conventional mindset would be to hire more office assistants, but what's the limit? One per meeting room? How long does this person take to put all the chairs back in order before the next meeting starts?

The answer was simple. This success could be easily achieved if every person who entered the meeting room would put their chair back in order. After illustrating this example, in the training I facilitated, I saw a change in the behavior of most people in the team. People who forgot to put their chair back in order before they left the room realized that their colleagues were doing it; therefore, they went back and helped. Even if a few people didn't do it, it didn't require a big effort for the rest of the team to put one more chair in order per person and to lead by example.

Why is this important? In an irreverent team, you never want people to think that certain things are somebody else's problem. Using the same principle of the chairs in the meeting rooms, we started a transformation to eliminate all manual quality assurance efforts in our software development process by stating that everyone should own quality, intentionally limiting the hours of manual testing that each team had available for their releases, and by promoting the prioritization of automation efforts that simplified the workflow and inviting more people to participate in the quality process regardless of their role.

The Software Engineer that started delegating the manual testing of the development to a QA Engineer realized that the quality of the code had much more impact in the speed of the release cycles than was earlier perceived. Although this impact existed before, the perception was diluted because everybody knew there was a defined stage of manual QA and it was normal to have a back-and-forth interaction with developers. This idea isn't new. Most of the successful native digital companies already work without assigned QA Engineers to do manual testing; however, too many teams in the world ignore this idea.

The bottom line of this step is that you should build the ownership culture in your irreverent team by starting from the small things and leading by example. No matter how fancy your office is, complacency is something you should never accept in the irreverent team.

The sixth and last step is to **reward success**. The good news here is that just by leading an irreverent team, you'll be providing the conditions for the people with the right sense of ownership to be motivated and develop a sense of realization that they wouldn't be able to achieve in an average company. Sometimes, this could be enough reason for someone to choose to work with you. One of the most negative emotional triggers is the sense of injustice; so, how could you expect somebody in your team to have a sense of ownership around a certain definition of success if the outcome for that individual won't be impacted by that success? Although this expected outcome is usually monetary, rewards can be broader than just a salary or bonus.

Almost every company implements some kind of bonus program to reward their employees beyond their normal salary when certain goals are achieved. Sometimes, they depend on individual objectives, and sometimes, there's also a company component. In the startup world and in many other companies, it's also common to witness distribution of shares or stock options. Whatever compensation strategy you choose, you should verify that achieving success at every stage will imply tangible rewards for everyone in the team, provided the individual expectations are also met.

I hope these six steps help you understand how to develop ownership within your irreverent team. Building an irreverent team isn't necessarily easy: Some of the behaviors that are represented don't change overnight, and some people even become blockers of these transitions. You'll probably have to make some tough calls, and these are muscles that you should train over time. What routine should you follow to keep doing the right exercises? In other words, what rituals should you put in place to create the perfect conditions for an irreverent team to develop? This is what we'll understand next.

KEY TAKEAWAYS

1. Segregating clear responsibilities makes people feel safe, but that's just an illusion in most Product Development teams. This approach doesn't reflect the real level of uncertainty that should be managed, and the business ends up paying a price, which reduces the real safety for everyone.
2. Get rid of internal contracts. Avoid having people defining what others should do and how. When you use SLAs internally, you're optimizing for average results. If your starting point is really bad, average can be okay for a while, but watch the behavioral implications closely.
3. Define your problem space and understand it. Present the challenges clearly, and hypothesize with your team about what's hindering the company's success. Most of the work

and results will derive from the right understanding of the problem space.

4. Treat adults like adults. Don't digest definitions for people: give everyone the chance to understand the full context, to contribute with ideas, and to challenge the decisions. Hold everyone accountable for having a critical perspective on what the team is doing and why it's doing it. If someone really prefers to be told what to do, they don't belong in an irreverent team.

5. Don't just trust. Verify. You don't need to be a chess master, but you must know the rules of the game to know when the checkmate is valid. Use a common understanding of KPIs to align what good work looks like in every case.

6. Overcome the fancy office bias. Don't accept that your team treats things as someone else's problem. Lead by example, even in the small things: clean your desk, and arrange the chairs when you leave a meeting room. Even if you work in a fancy office, don't let people feel that everything's already taken care of. That will easily be reflected in the everyday work.

7. Reward success. Find ways for people to feel recognized and rewarded when they contribute to overall success. Irreverents will want to work with you because of the irreverent nature of your team and the empowerment it provides; however, a sense of injustice will eventually be triggered if the right reward system isn't defined.

CHAPTER 6

STEP 4: DESIGN FEEDBACK LOOPS

Planning and organizing teamwork

How does your irreverent team define and organize the work to achieve success?

We've identified the connection between your definition of success, your objectives, the problems you should solve to achieve your objectives, and the solutions to these problems. But how do we navigate this process in practice?

When is the right time to talk about success?

How often should you define objectives, and when should you review them?

What should the team's workweek look like to balance problem-solving and solutions implementation?

How are any of these conversations conducted, and which spaces should be facilitated?

How will you know if the way you're organizing work is effectively successful?

I'd like to summarize all these questions as follows: How do you design the right feedback loops (your team's work cycles, your events, and your agenda) to learn continuously and succeed?

The strength of this idea relies on adopting the word *feedback* that will allow you to learn from the outcomes of your work and the environment. Moreover, the word *loops* represents the cyclical nature of the infinite game of business. Success isn't a place you arrive at; it's actually the constant exercise of shaping and impacting the reality around you in a way that's aligned with your core values.

What are the feedback loops in the business world that shape the way we work and organize today, and where do they come from? After reviewing this history and understanding the implications, I'll recommend the feedback loops you could design for your irreverent team.

The industrial mindset has a hierarchical and an asymmetrical approach to talent, where there's a management layer responsible for making decisions and defining the strategy, and an operational layer dedicated to executing what was defined by the management. A similar asymmetric approach happens with technical function–driven teams, where departments of the same company work separately. And some functions are responsible for defining what the other function should be working on. For instance, in this case you can see a Sales team trying to understand what the customer needs and defining the ideal product for the Engineering team to build. This segregated approach, which has been predominant in industrial-minded companies, still strongly influences how we organize teams in the Digital Age.

In industrial-minded teams, people in a specific position generate a list of projects or priorities to be executed by the rest of the team. What would be the conditions for this approach to work effectively? First, people responsible for defining the projects and priorities should have complete information and understanding on how to arrive at the right solutions. Second, the team responsible for execution wouldn't be able to provide any relevant contribution to the decision-making process. As I already stated, the issue is that these conditions almost never exist in the digital space.

ORGANIZING SOFTWARE DEVELOPMENT

Moreover, a new problem was introduced when companies started building digital products. In the process of building physical, manufactured objects, there is clear visual feed-back on the product's condition and the quality control is tangible, given than machinery and processes have been improving over decades. On the other hand, in the early years of digital products, writing software required a high level of abstraction and conceptualization, so when users executed the new software, it was difficult to know exactly what was happening behind the scenes; this is why any new piece of software was unstable. The code written to build applications relied on the developer's ability to abstract use cases into data structures, algorithms, and interfaces, and a lot of code had to be written before anything could be tangible for a user. The developer had to make many assumptions to build a software program; like any other human activity, it eventually introduced errors, incorrect assumptions, or bugs, which weren't identified till much later in the process. In some cases, fixing these issues required redoing a big portion of the work.

In 1970, Dr. Winston Royce wrote a paper titled *How to Implement Large Software Systems* in an attempt to solve this problem. He introduced what we term the 'waterfall methodology', which is based on identifying and separating six clear stages of the software development life cycle.

The first stage is the **requirements analysis**, where engineers had to understand and document any detail needed about the use cases that the application had to cover. The second stage was the **design**: in this case, the word 'design' refers to the software architecture, the data structures, and the integrations needed before writing any line of code. The third step was the **implementation** itself, which refers to how the engineers organized to write the code needed for the application. The fourth stage was dedicating time to **test** the application itself before releasing it to users. The fifth stage was the **deployment**, the process of making the application run in the production environment where real users operate. The last and sixth stage is **maintenance**: we ensure that the application runs smoothly, that any problem gets solved, and that new minor changes can be introduced as well.

Although the waterfall methodology has exhibited effectiveness in solving some project management challenges with strict deadlines and limited resources, in dynamic environments with some ambiguity, it wasn't effective at containing risks around the assumptions or errors introduced by the developers. This is why a big investment had to be made in the testing stage. The more we approached a demand-driven economy, the less viable the methodology became. Spending years to develop a software application wasn't competitive anymore.

In 1995, computer scientists Jeff Sutherland and Ken Schwaber presented the scrum methodology. After experimenting on different software development methodologies for many years during their careers, they were influenced by the Harvard Business Review paper 'The New New Product Development Game' published in 1986 and joined efforts to help the world simplify how software development was being done. The key innovation was the idea of working in much shorter iteration cycles and bringing different parts of the team together.

To accelerate decision-making and the adaptation to change, they introduced the role of the Product Owner who was in charge of aligning expectations with different stakeholders of the software project and arriving at clear definitions of what the team had to execute. It worked with an open product backlog of requirements that were frequently refined, and every sprint or iteration was used as the main source for the planning work. The prioritized work for a given iteration or cycle became the sprint backlog, with the intention of maximizing the chances of delivering a working software program at the end of every sprint.

They also introduced the idea of daily scrum meetings (a short meeting to check the progress of the sprint activities), sprint reviews (aimed at understanding and sharing the value delivered in the sprint), and team retrospectives (where the team reflected on how they worked during the sprint and how to keep improving). Scrum and its variations are the mainstream software development methodologies worldwide and are applied by most of the digital companies. In 2001, seventeen Software Engineers who were involved in the creation, experimentation, and testing of new software development methodologies met in a resort in Utah, USA, to define what was then known as the Manifesto for Agile Software Development, which is nowadays referred to as the Agile Manifesto. The engineers stated the values and principles behind what they believed to be a more effective approach to software development.

The values were as follows: individual interactions over procedures and tools, working software over comprehensive documentation, customer collaboration over contracts negotiation, and responding to changeover following a plan.

The principles were as follows: first, the highest priority is customer satisfaction through early and continuous delivery. Second, we welcome changing requirements. Third, we frequently deliver working software. Fourth, businesspeople and developers must work together. Fifth, build projects around motivated individuals, provide support, and trust their work. Sixth, the most efficient and effective form of communication is face-to-face. Seventh, working software is a primary measure of progress. Eighth, agile processes imply sustainable development and an environment where the team can maintain a constant pace. Ninth, continuous attention to technical excellence and good design improves agility. Tenth, simplicity is essential. Eleventh, the best architectures and designs emerge from self-organizing teams. Twelfth, reflect on how to become more effective at regular intervals.

When we hear about agile software development methodologies, we frequently think of scrum, extreme programming,

Kanban, or some combination of these, which align with at least part of the agile values and principles. Shortening the building cycles and adapting quickly to change implied a huge step forward for digital products. However, there's still a crucial part of the assumptions, principles, and practices that directly conflict with the digital irreverent philosophy.

When we say that the highest priority is to satisfy the customer through early and continuous delivery, who are we calling 'customer'? What are we delivering, and how do we measure satisfaction?

The digital irreverent doesn't accept calling somebody else who's performing a function at the same company or at a partner company 'customer' unless that person is effectively the end user of the product. Only after defining how we'll measure satisfaction, and how that relates to the common success, can we agree on the value of continuous delivery.

When we talk about welcoming changing requirements, who defines these requirements? As I explained before, there's an implicit or explicit authority that knows or pretends to know everything that should be built. The digital irreverent welcomes change, but doesn't welcome requirements. We understand the objectives, problems, and solutions, but not requirements, unless they effectively come from an authority that has a direct impact on the continuity of this product (e.g. a government regulator).

When we say businesspeople and developers must work together, where do we draw the line of who's business and who isn't? Is Sales business? Is Marketing business? What makes engineering or design not business? In the early days of Microsoft, was Bill Gates business or engineering? When

Larry Page and Sergey Brin founded Google, were they business or engineering? What about Elon Musk in Tesla, SpaceX, and his other endeavors—is he business or engineering?

The Digital Irreverent assumes that everyone is business and that regardless of your functional scope, you should be able to understand and make business decisions.

Last, when we say that working software is a primary measure of progress, how do we know that this working software will generate the business impact we expect? As I already mentioned, written code isn't an asset; it's a liability. The more problems we can solve in a sustainable way with less code, the more we can ensure the software development effort is aimed at the most crucial problems.

The bottom line is that to design the feedback loops (i.e., the working structure we need for our irreverent team), we have to disrupt the segregated decision-making that the current methodologies inherited. However, we still want to apply the valuable lessons that they provided around aspects like continuous delivery, building products around motivated individuals, the efficiency of face-to-face communication, the importance of being able to maintain a constant pace, continuously attending to technical excellence, and the potential of self-organized teams. Additionally, the most critical of all the aspects we want to keep is the practice of reflecting on a regular basis on how to improve and become more effective by sharing ownership across the team.

So, how do we solve the problem about the segregation of decision-making in an irreverent team?

We do that in the same way we explained in the previous chapter: through defining a common language across all teams on all levels. This common language is represented by objectives. Irreverent teams can expect the top management or founding leaders to define the high-level success (i.e., the goals derived from the massive transformative purpose or the company's mission).

The definition of success and the high-level goals are difficult to delegate to the team directly because they're completely dependent on the company's values and vision, and this is part of the critical path to defining the type of team you need (or even if you need a team at all). Once these high-level goals are defined, and you've surrounded yourself with the right motivated irreverents, the derived objectives can be delegated.

Delegation necessitates trust and support; however, in an irreverent team, the ability to verify that the right work is being done by talking frequently about the objectives and the results is crucial. This factor should be contemplated in the design of the feedback loops.

So, which feedback loops would I advise you to establish? By now, you should probably be familiar with the hierarchical relationship between:

1. the definition of success and the high-level goals,
2. the objectives and the key results,
3. the problem space, and
4. the solutions to these problems.

I believe each one of these four levels deserves its own feedback loop. Each level contains many feedback loops of the next level. In other words, you'll have many feedback loops to test solutions for given problems, many feedback loops of problems defined for the same objectives, feedback loops of different objectives being defined to achieve the same high-level goals, and maybe two or three feedback loops for defining success—if your organization lasts long enough.

My ideal feedback loop has five stages: planning, aligning, executing, reviewing, and reflecting.

Planning is related to understanding the assumptions, environment, and constraints related to the objectives at that level, and to defining and structuring the activities or the results needed from the next-level feedback loops.

Aligning means communicating what was planned, setting expectations for the rest of the team, and obtaining feedback to adjust anything that could've been missed.

Executing refers to the action itself, which entails solving the problem and executing the activities needed.

Reviewing means assessing the results of the objectives and their impact; it's focused on the 'what' and is also a space for alignment.

The **reflection** stage focuses on the 'how' (i.e., the decisions, behavior, biases, and patterns detected along the feedback loop), which impacts results or the team itself. The main objective of this stage is to learn and enter a continuous improvement mode.

Now, let's delve deeper into understanding the feedback loops at each level.

DEFINING SUCCESS AND THE HIGH-LEVEL GOALS

At a company level, this is probably a three- to five-year feedback loop. The planning is usually a business plan or an investor pitch depending on the stage of the company, and the alignment stage happens with the board and with the company's top management layer. The outcome of this alignment is usually shared with the rest of the team and with investors. An Executive team that embraces the digital irreverent philosophy is quite clear and transparent to their stakeholders about the things that they still don't know and about the assumptions they should make for the plan to succeed. However, they will be able to commit and to espouse confidence in their ability to learn fast and to solve the unknown variables using a systematic approach.

This business plan will probably fail at reflecting reality, and it will most likely be wrong as we delve deeper into the next level of feedback loops. However, the planning itself is key to defining a baseline and to initially shaping the following feedback loops. As Winston Churchill stated, 'Plans are of little importance, but planning is essential.'

I propose an annual review process. Your definition of success might not change, but the way you cascade the high-level goals might require an adjustment. It's also important to understand the evolution of the KPIs that derive directly from the MTP and to confirm that you're still heading in the same direction that you initially intended.

The reflection stage at this level can have different types of meetings (e.g. board meetings, top management retreats, etc.); however, big companies' transformations or restructuring activities are usually derived from these types of sessions. My objective in this chapter is to present the structure of the feedback loops; in Chapter 8, I delve deeper into the reflection stage.

CASCADING OBJECTIVES

This is commonly an annual exercise where we work with the three types of objectives we identified in Chapter 3. The first type can be expressed as follows: what derives from the massive transformative purpose beyond the short-term performance implications. The second type is the performance objectives that shareholders will mainly be concerned about. The third type are the enablers that should happen that year for the company to be on track, thus achieving success in the following years.

A combined example could be as follows: A, growing financial inclusion in the region by connecting one million new users to start saving through our app. B, achieving an annual operating revenue of $56 million. C, reducing fraud cases to 0.01% of the transactions.

Another set of objectives that can be classified under this level are the budgets. Some things are more important than others; that's why most of the companies usually summarize their yearly ambitions into five or six objectives. The most common practice entails reviewing these objectives monthly together with the budget, and maybe delving deeper every quarter to understand if certain decisions, specifically on how efforts are prioritized, should be made.

The reflection stage of this level should ideally happen right before the definition of the objectives for the next year.

THE DEFINITION OF PROBLEMS

For each yearly objective to be achieved, the irreverent team breaks it down into key results (usually between two and four KPIs and their targets); thus, when the KPIs are met, you're on track to achieving the objective. I prefer defining these key results quarterly and minimizing the changes in the teams during these terms.

The key results are, in fact, problems that have different levels of uncertainty and impact. The planning work beyond defining these key results entails breaking them into smaller problem hypotheses that we should test and solve to achieve the results. The key results and problem definitions can also be reviewed monthly, and I recommend having the reflection stage one or two weeks before commencing the next quarter.

WORKING ON SOLUTIONS

This title actually refers to bets or candidate solutions to the problems that were presented before. The solutions feedback loop should last between one and three weeks, which is very aligned with sprints (a scrum-derived term). The planning of these solutions implies prioritizing the candidate problems, depending on the level of impact and the level of certainty of that impact.

Subsequently, candidate solutions are identified and prioritized by certainty and impact. The irreverent team won't try to estimate the time that each candidate solution will take, but it will try to arrive at a combination of efforts that can drive the highest impact in the sprint or in the shorter time window defined.

The sprint review is the meeting where we assess the results of the sprint; this review enables us to understand the outcomes of the executed experiments and the direct impact of solutions rolled out as a consequence of having data-based evidence. The difference between the irreverent sprint review and the scrum sprint review is that we won't care that much about the functionalities delivered, but will care about the measurable business impact created and the concrete progress in our learning process. The effort dedicated to breaking down the quarterly key results, to understanding the problems deeper, and to elaborating the candidate solutions is also part of the work that should be planned during the sprint.

I usually try to ensure that at least 20% of the team's effort is dedicated to gaining more agility, which entails activities such as working on technical excellence, analyzing the data pertaining to previous experiments, and learning new technologies.

The reflection stage of this feedback loop is the sprint retrospective (i.e., the number one tool for building trust within the team), which we'll explore further in Chapter 8.

Although we've covered part of the first two levels of these feedback loops in the chapter dedicated to redefining success, it won't be the focus of this book to delve deeper into business plans or investor pitches. Navigating from the right objectives and key results to the underlying problems, and subsequently to the candidate solutions in an effective way, is the most frequent challenge that irreverent teams face and also where I believe I can contribute the most owing to my experience. This space for contribution is related to the ability of embracing uncertainty as part of the variables we can work with, which is the next area of focus.

KEY TAKEAWAYS

1. Founders and top management should define high-level goals based on their values and their MTP, but should also be able to delegate the definition of the next level of objectives to the team and coach them in the process.
2. Although building digital products requires embracing the complexity of software development, the first methodologies that were invented to manage this complexity, such as Waterfall, fail in the demand-driven economy because they're slow.
3. An agile approach to product development is key. We prioritize continuous delivery, building around motivated

individuals, efficient communication, continuous attention to technical excellence, self-organized teams, and
regular reflection.

4. However, not everything termed 'agile' is irreverent. We
welcome change, but not requirements. We don't call any
team Business: we're all Business. We value working software, but only if we can evidence impact related to our
objectives.

5. We organize nested feedback loops for defining success, cascading objectives, understanding problems, and
working on solutions. Each feedback loop should have
five stages: Planning, Aligning, Executing, Reviewing,
and Reflecting.

In the next chapter, which will be dedicated to embracing
uncertainty, I explain (in more detail) the decision-making
process associated with planning the feedback loops.

CHAPTER 7

STEP 5:
EMBRACE UNCERTAINTY

The competitive advantage
of irreverent teams

How do you connect your objectives with concrete actions that you can execute with your team? How do you formulate each action, and how do you prioritize them to achieve your objectives?

This is definitely not a new challenge for most organizations, and the industrial-minded companies have plenty of experience in cascading actions from objectives. You see a clear separation between the thinkers and the doers. A select group of senior managers strategize around projects that can drive the impact they need on the objectives. They identify the cost and the impact of each project and assign budget and personnel accordingly, thus facilitating the execution.

Of course, to be able to include the cost variable in that equation, some people in the group of the doers and some middle management had to invest time in providing estimations for the activities, people, and resources required in each project. The most experienced people in the group of the doers and middle management are wise enough to account for a big error margin: they know they'll be accountable for the timelines provided and the budget requested, even if they were very explicit on the risk implications of the estimation exercise itself.

Meanwhile, the most experienced group of the thinkers or senior managers are wise enough to identify ROI (return on investment) patterns, which entails stating, 'I will generate this amount of revenue after investing this much in this project.'

I believe that any industrial-minded company that exists today, at least once in its lifetime, produced something of enough value to their customers that they were willing to pay for it, and that the revenue they grew over time was probably the result of progressive gains in efficiency and of the optimization of this market relationship, and their approach to projects in a later stage is more incremental than existential. Thus, if they work effectively, they'll be able to generate a positive ROI; however, they won't be concerned with prioritizing high-risk bets that might reduce an existential threat for the business in the distant future, unless this risk is tangible in the short term.

By contrast, in the Digital Age, company extinction is almost always imminent, and the highest risk is *not* taking risks. As we already saw, for every given objective, there are many possible problems to address; and for each problem, there are also many possible solutions. Therefore, the irreverent leader perceives many contradictions between the industrial-minded approach and the contemporary approach or worldview.

First, there's a crucial difference between project management and product development. A project has a clear beginning and end, and its success is related to achieving certain results in a defined timeframe and not having to work on the same things after it ends. By contrast, a digital product has a clear beginning, but lacks a clear end. Desired results can be defined for specific timeframes, and if the product becomes successful, it will require many changes as we discover how users react to its evolution.

As we saw in Chapter 4, there will be teams with specific missions, which aim to achieve a result in the defined time window that's beyond a product and a technical function, such as migrating the system of an acquired company. However, most of your irreverent teams don't work in projects; they work in product development.

To achieve the high-level objectives, some product KPIs should improve, and the product development activity can't depend on a fixed set of solutions provided by the senior management.

The irreverent leader also sees no value in estimations. They usually require a lot of time and effort. They're generally wrong, and the reason for doing them isn't usually convincing. What exactly is an estimation? What would you need an estimation for? Is it because you should calculate some cost to prioritize this activity? In 2007, consultant Douglas Hubbard, author of *How to Measure Anything*, wrote an article for cio.com titled 'The IT Measurement Inversion': therein, he challenges CIOs and CTOs to check if they're deciding investments based on the right information. Douglas defines the value of information as the cost of being wrong, multiplied by the chances of being wrong; he further states that the objective of additional information is to reduce the EOL (expected opportunity loss), defined by the value of the opportunity loss multiplied by the chances of a loss occurring.

When analyzing the cost variable, he concludes: 'Even in projects with very uncertain development costs, we have found that those costs have an insignificant information value for the investment decision. In other words, information on the development costs did not lower the expected opportunity loss as much as information on other variables.'

The most important variables, those with the most uncertainty and impact on the decision, are rarely represented in the cost–benefit analysis, and Hubbard mentions that the single most important unknown variable is whether the project will be canceled.

The second most important unknown variable is the utilization of the product. This refers to how quickly it becomes available, and if somebody will use it at all.

The variables related to the projects being canceled, or the utilization of the system or product, indicate whether we're effectively solving the customer's needs, which we represented earlier as solving the problems that move the needle on the KPIs we defined.

We can accept cost as a constraint; however, the irreverent leader understands that this adds no value in the prioritization discussion, that the digital businesses play a very high ROI game, and that if you're trying to make a decision around an ROI lower than three digits, you'll be better off investing in real estate, the stock market, or crypto, rather than running a business in this space. (This is not investment advice.)

Every irreverent team also works with constraints in time and budget; however, instead of asking questions such as how much effort is required, what is the cost, or how long it would take to execute a predefined solution A, they ask a different question. The approach can be expressed using the following questions: Can we maximize the impact on this KPI within the next X to Y weeks, and how can I minimize the uncertainty about the problem I'm choosing to solve being the right one, and about the solution to that problem being the right one as well?

Irreverent teams utilize forecasts and frequent expectations alignments, but not intensive estimations. A forecast in this scenario is intended to provide the right order of magnitude around time and effort, with a very quick assessment of previous experiences and patterns that we already knew. However, this doesn't imply a detailed analysis of the efforts, nor involve too many people in the team to do this beforehand. It's like those famous interview questions: How many golf balls fit in a room, or How many piano tuners work in a certain city? The exact answer won't add value to any decision; however, there's a logical approach to providing an answer within the right order of magnitude in a matter of minutes.

The irreverent leader is driven by product development more than by projects, believes that there are many possible solutions to given problems and objectives and holds that the way to make the right decisions depends on the people who are closest to understanding the problem. The irreverent leader understands uncertainty and knows that the information about cost doesn't make any difference while making decisions on digital product development, and also that what moves the needle is collecting evidence confirming we're effectively solving the right problem. They understand that there's no point in working on estimations, and that they should instead focus on reducing uncertainty about the chosen problems, the candidate solutions, and on evidencing the impact of the simplest possible solution that can be executed in a short time window. However, when the irreverent leader reaches a state where some kind of time-line should be provided, they can provide a forecast within a matter of minutes.

ACKNOWLEDGING THE UNCERTAINTY

If you're pleased with this irreverent philosophy so far, I'm looking forward to discussing the method of connecting the objectives, problems, and solutions in the irreverent way. That's what the planning sessions that we discussed in Chapter 6 are reserved for. We'll delve deeper into the three levels of planning after defining the objectives. The planning meetings in scrum (and probably also in other so-called agile methodologies) assume that solutions are already defined. In the most favorable scenarios, they try to optimize the sprints, thereby providing an incremental value to customers within the given solutions. Contrastingly, the irreverent plannings rely on a predefined solution only if its results can be evidenced with data. These meetings are mainly focused on reducing the expected opportunity loss of the effort they're about to invest in the sprint.

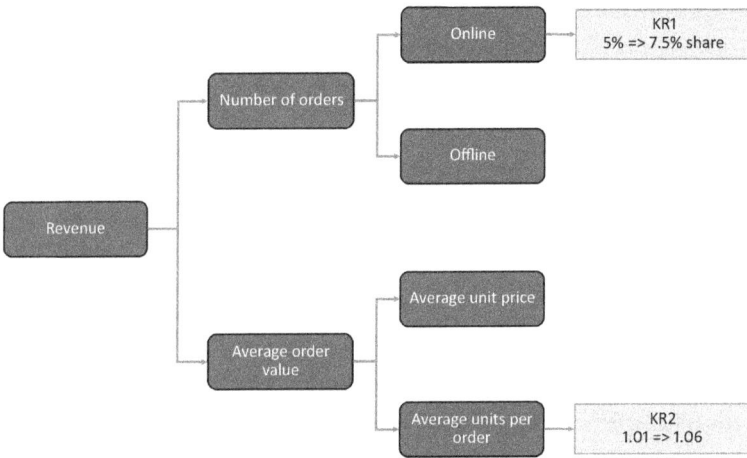

The first level of planning starts with the defined objectives and cascades the product KPIs, out of which certain key results will be prioritized. Let's illustrate this planning using the same example of the vegan bakery we defined in previous chapters. We assume that one of the bakery's objectives is to achieve $50 million in revenue by the end of the year. Therefore, we start drawing a value tree of KPIs. The first level of a tree has one node with the name 'Revenue'. The second level is broken down into two KPIs—number of orders, and average order value. In the third level, we break down the number of sales into online and offline channels, and also break down the average order value into two different KPIs, namely the price of the cake and the average number of cakes per order. (To keep this example simple, we won't go beyond the third level.)

Using available market information, we know that the price of our cakes is competitive, and that there's not much more space to increase it. We also know that the mix of online and offline sales in this industry is 40% online and 60% offline, whereas in our scenario, only 5% of the sales emanate from online channels. Although we have no information on the average number of items per order in the industry, our vegan bakery almost never sells more than one cake per order. By observing this value tree, we estimate that if we had something closer to our fair share of online sales, and if we could bundle a second smaller cake with 20% of our orders, we'd be achieving our revenue target for this year, and this is how we define (in this example) our key results for the first cycle or feedback loop.

LET'S CALL THIS QUARTER ONE.

Quarter One, Key Result One: Increase share of online sales from 5% to 7.5%.

Quarter One, Key Result Two: Increase the average number of cakes per order from 1.01 to 1.06.

Why did I choose these targets for the key results? A 7.5% share of online sales doesn't seem much compared to the 40% share of online sales that the industry shows, but this is a completely new problem for us, and we couldn't commit to improving this eight times without being able to assess the situation in significant detail. A 7.5% share represents a 50% increase from the 5% we initially had; so, if we find a way to keep growing this channel by 50% per quarter, it could represent more than a 25% share by the end of the year. Even if it's still behind the industry benchmark, the value might still be a reasonable target for a case we haven't yet explored. The same criteria apply for the increase in the number of cakes per order from 1.01 to 1.06. Even if this seems like a small number, if we achieve the same ~5% increase in the next three quarters, this same KPI could exceed 1.2 by the end of the year.

Why am I assuming that in every quarter I'll get the same performance improvement compared to the previous quarter on each KPI? Actually, that's not the main assumption. My primary assumption in these cases is that in my first cycle of attempting to solve these two problems, I'll be attaining between 10% and 20% of my calculated ceiling for these KPIs. In the case of online sales, my lowest ceiling is 40% (based on the benchmark), and I'm trying to move from 1/8 of the number share to less than 1/5 in my first attempt to solve the problem. In the case of average number of cakes per order, we don't have a precalculated ceiling; however, because we can calculate the number we should achieve to meet our overall objective, I assumed that every five orders will have more than one cake, which led me to an average of 1.2. After the first quarter, I'll have enough information to redefine the level of the ceilings, and thus redefine my key results, or even to choose completely new KPIs to focus on; however, we should start somewhere. Strong Product Managers, or strong Business or Strategy Analysts, are usually effective at conducting these key results plannings, which usually involve some research and a good understanding of the product's financial state.

The second level of planning has to do with prioritizing the right problems to achieve our key results. We start from the same value tree and break down the KPIs we chose in the previous planning into problem hypotheses, which can explain why the current level of that particular KPI is below our key result target. After conducting some research in our customer base and delving deeper into how our competitors operate, we listed some potential problems under the online sales channel.

1. Our website's payment gateway doesn't accept international credit cards.
2. All our competitors use delivery platforms as channels, and we don't.
3. Although we use one social media platform, others use three or four.

We also break down the KPI of the average number of cakes per order into candidate problems.

1. We learned that because some of the customers who buy a cake in our bakery are on their way to an event they're bringing the cake to, maybe it wouldn't be convenient to carry a second cake for later.
2. The team currently serving our customers at the bakery doesn't follow the practice of upselling: they don't offer customers the option of purchasing a second cake. They really don't know what could happen if they started offering more products.

Now, we have a list of five problems: three related to the share of the online sales channel, and two related to the average number of cakes per order. Using the same value tree structure, we could try to estimate the impact on revenue if each of these problems were true.

1. What would be the revenue potential if we had a fair share of international customers ordering online, compared to the number of international customers that come to the bakery?
2. What could be the revenue impact if we confirmed that 50% of the people in the neighborhood are only ordering through the delivery platforms?
3. What would happen if we could triple our website traffic by leveraging new social media platforms?
4. How many people do we believe would agree to buy a second cake if we decided to start offering this at the bakery?
5. What would be the revenue impact if we could offer customers the option of having the second cake delivered to their doorstep?

Although the exercise of defining key results implies some research and assumptions, remember that the idea isn't to find the exact numbers, but the relative order of impact of these problems. The second step of this planning is ranking the problems by impact, after which we'll assign to each problem a level of certainty, which indicates the certainty with which we believe that this is effectively a problem. In that case, how certain are we that it will generate the expected level of impact when it's solved?

For both dimensions, we can (for instance) use a scale ranked from one to five. We'll then plot these problems on a chart that combines the potential impact and the level of certainty. This way of visualizing the problems will be helpful for prioritizing them and subsequently defining the actions for the next level of feedback loops.

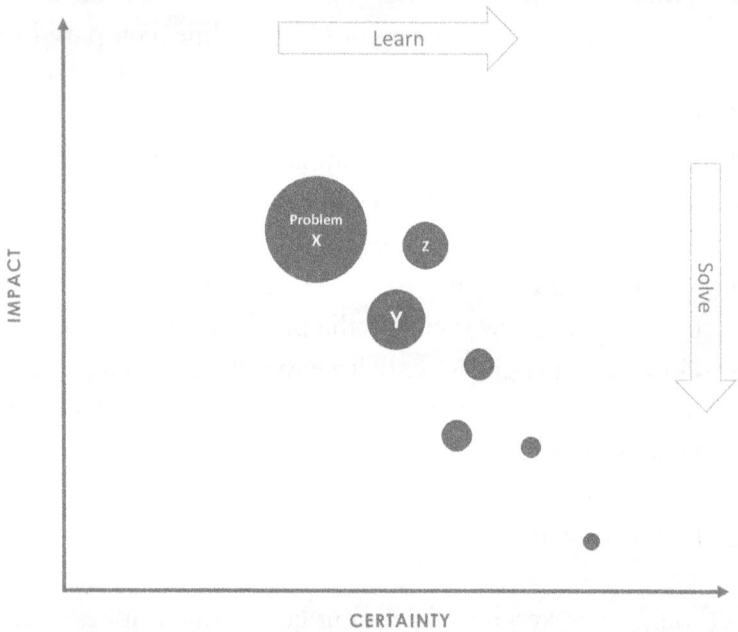

On the top right, we'll have high–potential impact and high-certainty problems. On the top left, we'll have high-impact and low-certainty problems. On the bottom left, we'll have low-certainty and low-impact problems, and on the bottom right, low-impact and high-certainty problems. When the team finds high–potential impact and high-certainty problems, they should stop doing whatever they're doing and focus only on those. That's the highest priority. High-impact and low-certainty problems represent the next level of priority, but not everybody in the team should participate in solving such problems. Although they usually require further research and analysis, these activities are also work that should be mapped. The low-impact and high-certainty problems will never gain priority over the last two cases; I, however, recommend dedicating between 10% and 20% of the effort in every cycle to address these.

This can be compared to the scenario of a person deciding to go to the gym. For most people, this won't be the main activity of the week, but if it's happening consistently over time, it can have a very positive compounding effect, and the opposite is true as well. If you never exercise, recovering from a health crisis in five or ten years can be much more difficult. Last, the low-impact–low-certainty problems can be ignored until new evidence shows us otherwise.

The problems prioritized out of this planning will be the input for the next and last level of planning: solutions planning. We'll go back to the value tree and try to cascade candidate solutions *only* on the problems we selected in the previous planning. Assuming we choose two problems that have a high impact and a high level of certainty, the following concerns are crucial:

1. Our team at the bakery isn't used to offering a second cake.
2. We aren't leveraging any delivery platform.

Our candidate solutions for the first problem can be expressed by:

1. Asking the team to start doing upselling,
2. Providing them with the sales training.

3. Hiring a different team, and
4. Changing the compensation structure to include a bonus impacted by the number of cakes per order.

We subsequently move to the problem related to the delivery platform. The solutions can sound something like this:

1. Integrate with Delivery Platform A.
2. Start offering your products on Delivery Platform A, together with a neighboring coffee shop that's already using it, and start leveraging the existing account with a good reputation and operational know-how.

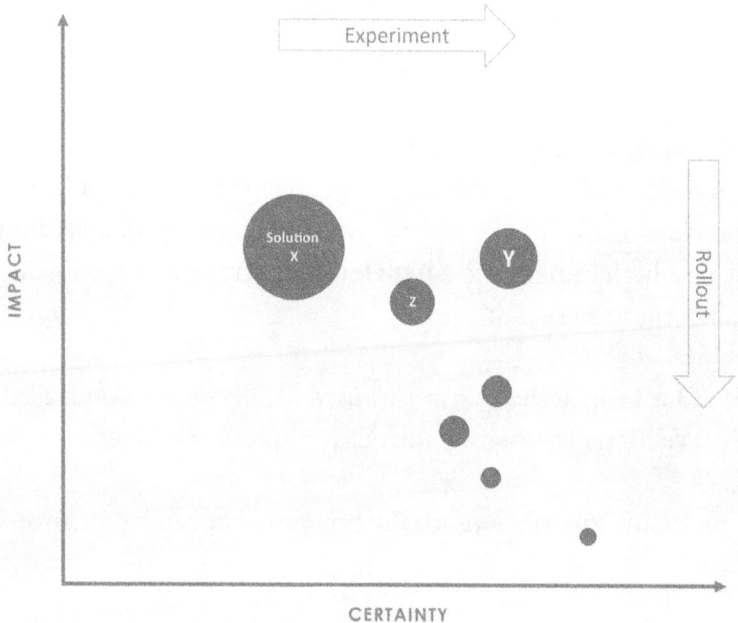

Now, similar to what we did in the previous level of planning, we'll rank these solutions by impact, understanding the position in the value tree and what part of the problem they solve. Subsequently, we'll rank them by certainty. Even when we said we don't like using estimation or costs as prioritization variables, a solution that inherently requires more work also implies a lower level of certainty. A team might end up perfectly executing all of these solutions, but the question here is: How do we prioritize them? Minimizing the expected opportunity loss at the solutions level is equivalent to ensuring that we're doing the most important thing. The high-impact and high-certainty solutions should simply be executed. The low-impact and high-certainty solutions will also apply the logic in the gym analogy by getting them done progressively with not more than 15% to 20% of the effort of each cycle.

The high-impact–low-certainty solutions will no longer be referred to as solutions. They will be termed hypotheses and can be expressed as follows: 'We believe Solution X will result in solving Problem Y. We'll have confidence to proceed when Z happens.' An example of this could be, 'We believe that integrating with the delivery platform will result in doubling our online sales. We'll have confidence to proceed when we sell an average of one cake a day during a week using our neighbor coffee shop account, which will leverage the existing integration.' This hypothesis can be tested through user research and through low-cost experiments on the product itself. Consistent with what we saw in the problem planning, low-impact and low-certainty solutions won't be considered.

WHAT SHOULD BE THE OUTCOME OF A SOLUTION PLANNING MEETING?

A solution should be a short list of experiments or discovery activities expressed as a hypothesis in the same way we saw in the previous example about the delivery platform integration. In this case, I'm also calling the solutions that we identified as high-certainty and high-impact experiments, a decision which can be explained as follows: Even if we have a high level of certainty, they're not effectively solutions until we've evidenced the impact. The number of experiments and discovery activities that will emanate from the planning will depend on what the team understands can be done in that cycle. As we saw earlier when we discussed estimations, the irreverent team will successfully break down experiments, discovery activities, and the development of solutions, thus evidencing (over one to three weeks) the impact generated in the key results within that cycle.

TAKEAWAYS

The most successful native digital companies are constantly running product experiments. They're running multiple versions of every product in parallel to learn and optimize for better results. In my experience, both the projects linked to the industrial mindset and the experiments we just described will have more than a 60% chance of failing to achieve the impact desired. The power of embracing uncertainty is that we optimize for the case of being wrong, which indicates that our failures are cheap. We get more attempts to generate impact in the same cycles, which maximizes the chances for our success. In fact, the irreverent leader also considers the team and the way of working as experiments, where in each case a certain hypothesis is set and the impact is evidenced, thus confirming if it was right.

That explains what we described earlier: Feedback loops are actually learning cycles. How do we make sure we also optimize for learning?

CHAPTER 8

STEP 6:
OPTIMIZE FOR LEARNING

Fail without suffering, and embrace
a culture of experimentation

What should you do when you know that most of your attempts to drive impact will fail? Why should you accept this statement at all, and what's the scary part about failing? I'll start by providing a straight answer to each of these questions.

When you know that most of your attempts to drive impact will fail, then you should optimize for the case of being wrong. That means reducing the cost of failing and avoiding the repetition of the same failures.

The reason you should accept the fact that most of your attempts to drive impact will fail is because you can't adapt to change in a demand-driven economy if you focus on only your high-certainty solutions. The moment you step into an uncertain territory of experimentation, most of the solution attempts will fail, and the certain solutions will be a small percentage of this group. The reason failing is scary is because most of our cultural and educational influences have taught us that you fail when you do something wrong, and when you do something wrong, it's bad and your tribe will reject you. In business and company terms, you might get fired. The irreverent leader solves these concerns by embracing a learning culture.

This chapter aims to propose an approach for optimizing for learning. Before stating my recommendations, let me unpack the fear of failure. Big manufacturers have learned to work with very sensitive profit margins, and defective products imply a waste of time, materials, machinery, electricity, and human work. Companies and whole industries have matured processes that minimize failures, and not following these processes would be irrational, considering the supply-driven economy where they were born. Any individual working at these companies who fails at executing these processes, either owing to incompetency or due to irreverence, becomes a direct threat to the business.

Any activity that requires any type of human action is prone to errors. Although some human errors are more justifiable than others, many industrial-minded companies have perfected the art of hiding problems and mistakes to avoid the justification headache. Due to the uncertainty of that justification being accepted or not, it became easier to hide mistakes hoping that they'll get diluted by an overall acceptable performance. This behavior feeds a vicious cycle where making any mistake becomes completely shameful and where no one wants to be exposed. Any company with this type of behavior will have a very difficult time adapting to change—and not adapting to change leads to death, which might be imminent if you're working in the digital space.

Many leaders in the digital space inherit management influences characteristic of the industrial mindset, where presenting problems and making mistakes isn't always welcome. As we discussed in Chapter 2, in the book *Outliers* by Malcolm Gladwell, the human communication challenges that emerged in tragic plane crashes reveal how much our cultural influences in behaving, communicating, and deciding can lead to very negative outcomes. For many individuals, the way they assimilated family education, country or community culture, or religious values may deeply condition the emotional experience when making mistakes—including the emotional experience when the person realizes that other people perceive these mistakes and when they see others making mistakes. To drive a learning culture, you first should face the fear of failure.

If you're a startup founder, you've already come a long way in the journey of embracing uncertainty and the fear of failure; however, most of the jobs we know today rely more on executing on a known path, applying proven solutions, and implementing processes that already exist. In these cases, my proposed statement (that most of your attempts to drive impact will fail) is incorrect, because it's only about attempting efforts on the safe path; however, this impact might not be enough at some point. If you zoom out, the success of many companies, industries, and even humanity has always depended on people that have a strong inclination towards exploring new possibilities. This even goes beyond adapting to change; it's about human curiosity, which facilitates exploration and discovery.

What's the value of traveling to many places in the world versus going to the same beach resorts that you already know? What's the value of exploring new restaurants or food instead of eating at the places you already know and like? As Marty Cagan from the Silicon Valley Product Group introduced in his 2008 book *Inspired*, product development is effectively an activity driven by exploration, a constant attempt at offering your customers valuable, feasible, usable, and viable solutions. Valuable means that your customers perceive value in your product, and that they're willing to use it or even to pay for it. Feasible is related to the ability to build this product (Does the technology and knowledge to build this exist?). Usable represents the easiness of use by your user or customer. For instance, computers weren't usable for most people before icons and friendly user interfaces were created.

Finally, viable means that it's reasonable for the organization to invest in building this product, and generally relates to an expectation of future profit. Successful products that tick these four boxes were never created like this on the first attempt. They're the result of experimentation and of understanding the empirical evidence required to identify what's valuable for their customer, achieved by overcoming the fear of failure.

The best antidote for fear is curiosity, and this is what opens the possibility of discovering unexplored paths. In Chapter 7, I proposed that executing low-impact–high-certainty activities was comparable to going to the gym or exercising, that doing this consistently would compound over time and accelerate the impact of the other solutions, and that you should probably dedicate between 10% and 20% of your solution feedback loop to these activities.

But what's the right dedication for exploration or experimentation? In 2016, computer scientists Brian Christian and Tom Griffiths launched a book titled *Algorithms to Live By,* where they dedicate a chapter to the exploitation versus exploration problem. How long should you spend exploiting the options that you already discovered versus exploring new options? They explain that the most crucial variable in this case is time. What's the time window you're optimizing for? The shorter the time window you're optimizing for, the less exploration you want to do. How open would you be to the idea of trying a new restaurant this weekend in your city, compared to trying a new restaurant on the last night of your vacation in a place that you've already identified as your favorite restaurant? The way this analogy translates to the challenge of building digital products is that we already know that new restaurants are constantly being opened; therefore, exploration is a necessity.

Subsequently, the authors present the idea that the algorithm we utilize for this problem is the one that minimizes the pain of regret, defined as the result of comparing what we actually did with what would've been best in hindsight. As you already know, in the irreverent philosophy, the highest risk is not to take risks. Finally, the authors conclude that the best approach for this problem is being optimistic because (A), we can go back to the high-certainty option later, and (B) every attempt to explore will potentially provide us with learnings about how to explore better. This is referred to as the accumulation of knowledge, which is described as follows: It's rare that we make an isolated decision where the outcome doesn't provide us with any information that we'll use to make other decisions in the future. In other words, failure will lead to better exploration- and exploitation-related decisions. That's why we should be efficient at failing.

To illustrate how you can reduce the cost of failing, we can again use the bakery scenario. Let's suppose that your business is doing okay by selling three types of cakes; however, you're trying to achieve higher objectives for next year, and you believe that introducing a new type of cake may increase your sales. Assuming this is a good hypothesis, how do you test a new cake? You can adapt the production process of your bakery to incorporate this fourth type of cake, purchase all the ingredients, and start baking at the same scale of the other three types, hoping it will sell even more than the others.

A possible way of reducing the cost of failure is baking a small batch of cupcakes with the same flavor and offering them to the customers that buy the other cakes. We might try selling a larger batch of cupcakes the week after if the feedback is good; depending on the number of sales of those cupcakes, we might choose to start baking cakes of the same flavor, then increase the production according to the sales trend. This cupcake analogy is well known in the lean community; it explains how to achieve value for your customers in a lean way, which implies finding the minimal version of the product you'd like to test that's enough to confirm your hypotheses. Failing to set up a cupcake sampling routine is much cheaper than failing to set up a completely new cake production line. The same analogy can be applied to digital products. For instance, at Quicko we routinely tested new experiences on the mobile app by rolling out changes only for some Android users; later, we developed or adapted the iOS version once the hypotheses were validated. In some cases, it's probable that the users' preferences and behaviors might change depending on the device; however, this example makes sense for that context.

Let's now imagine a more complicated scenario where you don't even have the cake shop. You do have the business, but you bake your cakes at home. You sell your cakes in a farmer's market, where you put up a stand every weekend. How long will it take you, in that scenario, to define a new cake flavor if that's your only sales channel? What happens if on one of every four weekends, it rains and nobody shows up? In the Software Engineering world, most teams probably release changes in their digital products via a dynamic that's closer to the farmer's market example. A lot of preparation and certain conditions must occur to be able to release every one or two weeks, and in some cases, every month or even every quarter. How much should I invest in experimenting with new features or changing the user experience, when each iteration takes a couple of weeks?

The best teams in the world apply continuous delivery: They apply practices of quality automation, continuous integration, continuous deployment, and a progressive approach to rolling out the changes, where users aren't impacted all at once, and there's initially a controlled version being presented on top of which we can compare the impact of the new change we released. This also includes the ability to switch this feature off in case something goes wrong. Industrial-minded companies release their digital products once every few weeks at best, minimizing failures. However, the best digital-minded companies release multiple versions of their digital products many times a day, minimizing the cost of failing and thus maximizing learning.

To minimize the chances of repeating failures, you should embrace a learning culture that promotes a systematic way of learning out of every experience, and also an effective communication strategy to ensure we learn from each other's mistakes as well. An effective learning culture starts by figuring out a way of letting everybody know that mistakes won't be punished, and that the act of making existing problems visible will even be rewarded; however, this will only be effective if it can be perceived in the actions and not only in the messages. I once heard a definition of culture that defined it as how people behave when others aren't watching. In this case, it's not about pretending not to care about mistakes, but about deeply caring about the learning.

One of my favorite tools to determine how to learn from failures is producing a post-mortem document or meeting after the failure or the incident happened, which entails answering four questions.

1. What happened? The answer to this question provides a description of the incident of failure and the context in which it happened.
2. What was the impact of that failure? Did we affect users? Did we affect an operation? Is this quantifiable in terms of revenue, cost, or through any business KPI?
3. How did we learn about this? Did we learn about this failure because a client called us? Were we proactively monitoring the performance of a product? Did we receive any system alerts?

4. What are we going to do to minimize the chances of this happening again? Apart from trying to minimize the chances of future failures, improving how we measure impact and how we're informed when things happen is crucial for a learning culture.

When we consider the feedback loops we learned in Chapter 6 and interpret them as learning cycles, we identify three dimensions of learning. The first dimension is the What. What solution experiment worked? What didn't work? What was the impact of a problem being solved? Which objectives have we achieved, and how close are we now to what we defined as success in the beginning? This dimension is addressed by the review stage of each feedback loop.

The second dimension is the Why. Once we identify the solution experiments that failed, the problems that ended up being less important than we believed, and the objectives that we missed, we start asking why as many times as we need to. We should understand what we missed and why we missed that. Did we miss something in the execution? Did we miss something in the understanding of the problem? Once again, how can we minimize the chances of making the same mistake in the next feedback loop? Or if it wasn't a mistake, how can we update our objectives and prioritize problems or candidate solutions to reflect the reality we understand right now? This dimension is managed by the reflection stage, and the way I recommend running it is by going back to the value tree, where we cascaded the problems and the solutions, and trying to answer the Why next to every solution and problem explored that didn't reach the expected impact. Ideally, we should ask 'Why' two or three times in every case (i.e.: Why didn't solution X work? Because we didn't consider Y. Then, why didn't we consider Y?), until we reach the root cause and can find actionable learnings.

The third dimension is the How: How are we operating as a team, how aligned are we, how motivated and engaged do we feel, and what's stopping us from becoming the type of team we want to be? This dimension is usually driven by retrospectives. We discussed retrospectives in reference to scrum, and there are many types of ceremonies such as this one. One simple and effective retrospective approach, especially for starting teams is the keep, fix, try retrospective, which works best when you have some clarity of your objective as a team: Each member of the team writes four cards without showing them to anybody. Two will have one point each of something that went well in the last feedback loop (things that we believe contributed to becoming the team we want to become). The other two will have one point each of things we want to fix to achieve the same purpose.

After giving a few minutes for everyone to complete their cards, we let each member of the team present the cards briefly and let the members paste each one in the right column, Keep and Fix. The moment of sharing the content of the card should be brief, and only questions for clarifications are allowed. This isn't a good moment for debate because each one is presenting their perceptions, and perceptions aren't debatable. This is also a crucial dynamic to not let extroverts dominate the meeting. As people keep presenting their cards, closely related points in each column from different people can be pasted together.

Subsequently, there's an acknowledgement of the main point to 'keep' because they went well, and there's a vote on the top points that we'd like to fix. After defining the top two or three points that we'd like to fix, we align together one objective for each chosen point, and write them in the 'try' column. Each try item will be led by volunteers in the team to achieve an action plan before the next retrospective meeting. There are multiple types of retrospective meetings that present variations of the aforementioned one, and the irreverent leader also experiments on which retrospectives work best for each team and each maturity stage.

We talked about the What, the Why, and the How, but we also have a fourth dimension called the Who, which is related to the individual performance and cultural alignment of each person in the team. What was expected from this person in this last feedback loop? What was their contribution towards the team's impact? Did the person share ownership? The irreverent leader focuses more on people than on processes and knows that a learning culture is also a feedback culture.

In 2017, Kim Scott launched a book titled *Radical Candor*, which became one of the most important references of how to approach feedback. The phrases that summarize the spirit of the book are 'care personally' and 'challenge directly'. The irreverent leader understands that caring personally about each team member is fundamental to sharing ownership. Challenging directly provides clarity, and if done respectfully, can drive inclusion because every person can have different interpretations when reading between the lines, and an unintended impact can be generated. However, a direct challenge can be immensely appreciated when it's delivered with care.

I believe that at least for each of the feedback loop levels, solutions, problems, and objectives, every team member deserves a gift. That gift is the feedback conversation that will help that team member get closer to their career objective.

First, we listen to the team members' understanding of the impact each of them is generating in the feedback loop. Second, we calibrate the same points with our perception as leaders based on evidence. Third, we acknowledge and discuss the gaps, if any, between the expectations of the role and the impact effectively generated in that feedback loop. Fourth, if needed, we agree on a behavioral adjustment which should be the focus point for maximizing the chances of achieving the desired impact in the next cycle. When you truly embrace a learning culture, every practice and process is subject to change, and irreverent teams change it from the bottom up. In the end, everything is aligned by the same definitions of success, and high-performing autonomous teams figure out the best way of working by focusing on continuous improvement.

TAKEAWAYS

1. Irreverent teams should overcome the fear of failure and embrace a learning culture, where mistakes aren't punished but exposed with the mandate to learn from them collectively. Post-mortem meetings and documents are excellent tools for this.

2. To survive in the digital space, we should continuously invest efforts in exploring new paths. Optimism towards exploration is a winning strategy that accelerates learning and improves decision-making.

3. To accelerate learning, we should fail quickly and cheaply: we should be able to constantly run product experiments that validate our hypotheses with the smallest investment possible and in the shortest time window. Enabling continuous delivery and the right data analytics tools is key. Once we confirm our hypotheses, we can confidently invest more in scaling the successful solutions.

4. For every feedback loop, have meetings with your team to review the What, question the Why of the missed results, and reflect on the How using the retrospective template that better suits you.

5. For every feedback loop, also ensure that everyone in your team has a dedicated 1:1 conversation to reflect individually about their contribution in the loop and about the expectations for the next cycle.

Does this mean that you have all you need for your irreverent journey? What about your own irreverent preparation? What do you believe it takes to become an irreverent team member? What scares you about this path?

CHAPTER 9

EMOTIONAL IRREVERENCE

Preparing your emotional wiring
for the irreverent journey

How irreverent do you think you are today?

What are the implicit and explicit authorities that guide the way you work?

What type of connection do you feel between the work you do and your individual purpose?

Using the reference from the book *Outliers* in the chapter dedicated to plane crashes, what would you do if you had the chance to travel in time and meet five years before the accident with the co-pilot of the plane? What would you say to this person? What recommendations would you give?

Fortunately, for most of us, none of our decisions at work imply life or death situations. But in a certain aspect, most of us are also like this co-pilot. We go through different situations where we avoid making decisions, stepping up, challenging authority, or taking the lead when we don't perceive that this depends on us. In contrast, the irreverent journey is a journey of fulfillment. You're constantly trying to work on what you believe is right, and when you see the actual impact of your efforts, you feel more empowered and keep feeding the cycle by trying to improve more things around you. I would even risk saying that irreverent leaders and irreverent teams enjoy work, and maybe life, more than conventional leaders and teams.

BUT WHY IS THE IRREVERENT JOURNEY DIFFICULT?

We all inherit values and beliefs in our adult lives, which are derived from family, the type of education we received, and the culture around us. These values and beliefs are generally not designed to maximize the impact around you, but to keep you safe or even to keep others around you safe—even if the potential threats on which the beliefs are rooted don't exist in your current reality. This chapter aims to acknowledge the emotional implications of starting the irreverent journey and to give you tools for separating the real risks from the fears that exist only in your mind and to deal with them.

Now, let's dissect the notion of beliefs and values.

Beliefs are the stories you bear in your mind—stories about how the world works or about how the world should work, which were either transmitted to you or created by your mind out of experiences you had. *You should always tell the truth to your parents. If you don't share, you won't have friends. You should always respect your teachers. If you smoke, you'll die young. For your family to be proud, you should become a doctor or a lawyer. Build your career at a big company, and you'll do well in life. Businesspeople care about the What. Engineers care about the How. To make money, you should work really hard. Money is the root of all evil.* These are just examples of stories that we tell ourselves. Some of them might be right, while others might be wrong. Some occupy deeper spaces in our mind where we can't identify them that clearly: they can always remain strong without needing any real-world evidence.

Values are our moral compass. They form the basis of our logic in regard to what's right and what's wrong, what's good and what's bad, and what I can accept and what I can't accept. They shape our personal interpretations of ideas such as justice, respect, truth, freedom, family, and responsibility. We can't objectively say that certain values or beliefs are good or bad, because we'd always be calibrating them with our own value system. However, we can try to understand if they're aligned or misaligned with different environments and cultures.

Many years ago, at a leadership retreat at Mercado Libre's offices in Buenos Aires, we had as a guest speaker a professor from Stanford University who discussed the challenges related to culture in a multinational company. He presented a hypothetical scenario of two friends in a car. One of them is driving at 15% above the speed limit. The car runs over a pedestrian who crossed the street without looking. The police arrive and start questioning the friend in the passenger seat. How would this scenario play out if these two friends were Americans in the US, versus if the two friends were Argentinians in Argentina?

Relying on stereotypical assumptions, the professor says that the friend in the US, proud of his moral standards, would tell the police that his friend was speeding and would let the judge decide the right action to take, and that the friend in

Argentina, also very proud of his high moral standards, would never betray his friend and would lie to the police about the speed at which the car was driving. What's more important to you—the approach to justice in the transit law of your city, or seeing your friend in jail for a mistake he made?

VALUES ARE SUBJECTIVE

The answer will depend on your values. My interpretation around these types of comparisons is that every culture has its own way of calibrating the hierarchy between the individual, the family, the community, and some abstraction of a much larger group of people (e.g. a city, a country, a religion, a sports team, or a political party). Without trying to classify your values as good or bad, we can maybe understand what hierarchical combination they're optimizing for. I believe that the American friend is optimizing for the proper functioning of this abstraction of a larger group, which might be a city, a state, or a country that relies on clear transit laws to benefit most of the people in that group. On the other hand, the Argentinian friend is optimizing for the 'family and friends' level. Continuing with the stereotypical assumptions, the Argentinian might feel that his friends will always be there for him in any type of situation, but might not necessarily rely on the city, a state, or the nation for his security and his needs, and might not value the functioning of that structure over the loyalty of the friendship.

Nobody can ask you to change your values. Unless you go through a very intense emotional experience, you can't assume that your values will change. That's why the irreverent journey can't be detached from your values. You should work at a place where you don't feel that your core values are compromised. Meanwhile, your beliefs are easier to change. If you decide to dedicate the work to unpacking the stories behind them, remember that they exist in the first place to protect you from feeling something that you don't want to feel. The biggest threat to the irreverent journey is the fear of being expelled from a group or community, which in evolutionary terms made a lot of sense: it prevented our ancestors from being left alone in the forest and being eaten by wild animals or killed by other tribes.

But can these fears be justified today? What are the things that we're not willing to feel that are based on deeply held beliefs which are no longer useful? Many examples of beliefs that aren't useful are related to money and wealth. Since the success of the book *Rich Dad Poor Dad* by Robert Kiyosaki in 1997, many people started questioning their beliefs around money and investing. Consequently more literature has been published about the difference in the mindset of rich people compared to everyone else. There are even stories of people who succeeded in their wealth accumulation journey but seemed completely irrational when making decisions about spending.

Like the case of a billionaire who was driving twenty additional minutes a day to find a gas station with lower prices. Have you heard of people who want to have more money but espouse habits around saving, investing, and spending that are completely inconsistent with this statement?

There could be many different explanations for this behavior. Some people might not really value money. Other people might even have this as a clear goal, but their belief system could be triggering a sense of guilt when they start accumulating wealth. Some people might have a strong belief of what's the right way of making money and the way which they choose gives them much less than they really need to fulfil their goals. Some people might have a compulsion around spending (that might also be preventing them from feeling something else which they don't want to feel). But the most difficult part is that money doesn't mean anything by itself. If we don't have the ability to accumulate it and manage it towards a feeling we want to have in the future or a purpose, we'll find it hard to drive the changes in our beliefs. In other words, the number in your bank account is just a number. What's your target number, and what will this number endow you with?

Your target feeling can range from safety to independence to freedom to power to gratitude or even to the excitement about having achieved one more goal. The reason I like to use this example about money is because it's very easy to perceive. You see all ranges of behaviors around spending, saving, investing, talking, or even not talking about this topic because in most cases, it triggers emotions related to deeply rooted beliefs. This is even considered to be the number one reason for people getting divorced. So, how can we build a similar case for the fear triggered by challenging authority? What type of emotions get triggered in you when you explore ideas such as quitting your job and starting your own business? These ideas may include telling your boss that you disagree with some decision, explaining to the team that the process you're following doesn't make any sense, questioning the purpose of the project you're working on, or presenting a pitch to a potential investor when you have no experience.

SENSE OF BELONGING

The reason I mentioned the fear of getting expelled by the tribe is because the most common worst-case scenario in any of these examples is losing your job. In many cultures, probably in yours as well, your job and the work you do are closely related to your sense of identity. Who are you in this world, in this community, and in your group of friends when you don't have your job? For many people, losing a job also means putting their safety at risk, not being able to pay rent, or even not being able to provide for their families. Some might even be living in a country on a working visa and losing their job might compel them to leave the country and leave behind the life they built there.

Here, you see the Maslow Pyramid at play. You can't pursue your self-actualization and fulfil your irreverent journey if your self-esteem is low, if you don't have a sense of belonging in a social or a family environment, if your physical safety is at risk, or if you don't have the means to obtain food and shelter. Let me present a strategy for overcoming this fear using four steps that work across the Maslow pyramid. For each step, ask the following questions: How can I know if this risk is real? If it *is* real, how can I mitigate that risk now? If it eventually happens, what's the best plan I can think of right now to get out of that situation? First, how can I know that if I lose my job, I won't be able to **pay for food and shelter** and provide for my family? Do I have savings or other income? How long can I stay afloat till I find my next job? If this risk is real, can I think of new sources of income?

Can I lower my expenses today to grow my savings? Can I learn more about unemployment insurance or government programs? If I effectively lose my job and am not economically prepared, can I talk to my landlord to get a rent exemption for a couple of months? Can I move in with a family member or friend? Can somebody in my family support me for a few months? These scenarios sound a little bit extreme for the tone of this book, but if you can train your mind to prepare for the worst-case scenarios, your situation will definitely be much easier than the one I'm describing. In 2015, Elon Musk shared with Neil deGrasse Tyson in the podcast *StarTalk* the story of how he lived for a period of time with $1 a day when he was a 17-year-old college student in Canada. He explained, 'My threshold for existing was pretty low, so I figured I could be in some dingy apartment with my computer and not starve.' Without a doubt, he was preparing for his irreverent journey. He was testing the minimum viable conditions in which he could spend his time in a way he could maximize his impact.

Moving to the second level of the pyramid. If you lose your job, how can you know this will significantly affect your **sense of belonging and your social life**? Who are you outside of your job? Who are you in your family? Do you practice any sport activity? Do you study or teach at some school or university? Are you part of an online gaming community? Who are you as a friend? If you lose your job and your sense of belonging is at risk, how can you mitigate it? How can you ensure you have a balanced life outside of your job? What moments in your week can you dedicate to nourishing your relationship with your family, with your friends, or even finding spaces for meeting new people?

If you lose your job, your sense of belonging is dramatically affected, and you haven't prepared enough for that. What can you do then? Can you invest part of that potentially available time in connecting with friends and family, or in exploring new activities where you can meet people? Do you know of any coach or therapist who can potentially provide help in navigating difficult times? In 2017, I was working at Mercado Libre, and I moved from Chile to Brazil to help with a potential acquisition of a company in São Paulo. It was going to be my second time relocating for work, and I had no friends or family in the country apart from some people I knew at work. I learned from my experience in Chile that when you relocate, you end up having a lot of time for yourself. In the beginning, you have an empty agenda outside of work, without friends or family commitments and you can choose between planning how to spend this time or relying on your mood when you get back from work to see if you watch some videos, check your emails, or whatever you feel like doing.

So, when I arrived in Brazil, I decided to plan my free time outside of work in a meaningful way. That year, I started studying Chinese and practicing yoga. I wasn't having the best time at work during my first few months in Brazil, as I was waiting for a company acquisition to be confirmed so I could work on the integration. But in the meantime, I didn't have much to do. I'd left my previous role in Chile, and I basically had a salary but no job until the acquisition was confirmed. Ironically, those first months in Brazil ended up becoming an inflection point in my life. I began my immersion into the Brazilian culture, discovering São Paulo and its amazing diversity, becoming fluent in Portuguese, and being disciplined with the activities I'd planned. I haven't attained a satisfactory level of fluency in Chinese, but I learned so much more than I'd ever imagined.

Yoga ended up becoming an essential part of my life and of how I see the world around me. It helped me shape a completely new lifestyle that I adopted for good and even improved my level of conditioning for the rest of my activities. That same December in 2017, when I started learning Chinese and practicing yoga, I also met the person who became my wife years later. This could've just been a coincidence, but I don't know what would've happened if my sense of identity had depended on who I was at work during that time. This second step of the strategy is also related to your self-esteem. So, while working on the points I mentioned earlier will help grow your sense of confidence, you can't neglect your mental and physical state. Your daily habits—namely how you eat, how you sleep, how you think, and how you rest—compound over time and have a huge influence in your daily life.

The third level is related to the self-actualization and starts by asking: How can you know if your job **was effectively the best way to drive your purpose** and that you'd be throwing away that chance if you lost it? Is it effectively the most important space to connect with your aspirations? How can you be sure of this? What are you comparing this experience with? If for some reason this job is effectively your calling in life, how can you mitigate the risk of losing it? Can you connect with the same purpose in other spaces besides work, universities, meetups, events, and content creation? Where would you be working, if not in this place? Would you start a company of your own? Is there anybody in your network doing something that also resonates with your purpose?

My passion is to help leaders in Product Development teams to augment their impact. I was and am absolutely motivated about doing this at work; but I knew that at some point there were conditions that didn't depend on me to influence how this transformation could keep expanding along the organization. I also realized that I couldn't scale my impact enough by only doing this at work. Therefore, I started writing this book. If for whatever reason, at some point I stop transforming leaders and Product Development teams at work, if at least I can help a person or a team somewhere transform their perspective about product development through this book, I will have fulfilled my purpose beyond my expectations.

The fourth step entails **questioning the evidence that justifies this fear** head-on: How can you know if your job is effectively at risk? Do you really think that challenging the status quo, questioning the objectives, or presenting a new way to organize a team or whatever irreverent attitude you have will influence someone enough to fire you? Probably not. Then you can make a decision using the framework of minimizing regret. Between Options A and B, what would your 80-year-old self, regret doing? And what option would disappoint your 10-year-old self? Remember that not acting and not making a decision is also making a decision: again, sometimes the highest risk is not to take risks.

In 2019, after fourteen years at Meli, I decided to leave the most important and prestigious digital company in Latin America to join a very early-stage startup in the mobility space in Brazil called Quicko. I was offered a hybrid position that merged the Chief Product Officer and Chief Technology Officer roles. The previous Chief Product Officer had resigned three months before I joined, and the last Chief Technology Officer exited one month later. Most of my friends and family advised me to stay at Meli, and I had enough evidence to believe that Quicko could potentially fail within a year. However, when I ran this decision through the Regret Minimization Framework, I knew this would be a unique chance to test my skills in a new environment and that my first year at Quicko would be much more rewarding than my fifteenth year at Mercado Libre. I was even prepared for it to last only six months. My two-and-a-half years at Quicko ended up being some of the most fulfilling in my career, and that experience potentiated my opportunities around the world.

Once you go through these four steps, the only thing left is to decide and commit to the decision you made. Instead of the fear of losing your job, you can play the same strategy with different types of fears, which include not getting the promotion or the salary you expected, upsetting somebody you fear, feeling rejected by your team, or any other fear you can imagine. The real irreverent doesn't care too much about the job title or about small differences in salary increments. The job title only matters if it conditions your ability to drive the maximum possible impact. But most of the time it doesn't: It's how you behave that matters. On salary increases, they'll probably never be important enough to build your wealth or help you achieve your ultimate goals related to money. They're usually a good symbol for recognition. The digital irreverents find their strategy to achieve financial independence through investing and exploring new sources of income, not only at work.

Far from distracting you from your main job, having at least some financial safety will provide you with the right level of confidence to be as irreverent as you need. That is, of course, if you're not willing to live on $1 a day like Elon Musk did at college. One recommendation that I'd like to give you is not to take things too seriously. Most of the emotional limitations you probably have derive from the stories and beliefs that you take seriously. The four-step strategy I presented before is effectively to gain perspective on how your fears inform your decisions, which in the end has the same intention of not taking things too seriously. Gamify your experience, and ask yourself the following question: What would be the attitude of the irreverent version of yourself in that same scenario?

Some people who go through important transformations in their lives even symbolize this by changing the way they dress, the way they talk, and maybe even the way they walk. So, feel free to use any tool available to symbolize your irreverent transformation. Don't forget that people around you, especially non-irreverents, will also react with their own emotions triggered by fears, beliefs, and values. My recommendation is that you approach these situations with genuine curiosity. How can you ask them to walk you through their reasoning? What is the story they're telling themselves to feed a certain belief?

If you're starting this journey and you're in a hostile environment, and if regardless of your efforts, things don't seem to flow, evaluate changing your context and doing this somewhere else. Sometimes, coaches and mentors can help you navigate through difficult team dynamics, having conversations with other leaders, and gaining a practical perspective on many of the things we observed in this chapter. But the most important factor in the irreverent journey is that once you're on it, you can't go back. Once you've worked with an irreverent team, you'll never want to be telling people what tasks to do at work—just as you won't accept others telling you what to do after you've felt the potential of your own empowerment. But you should always respect that everyone's in a different part of the journey, and each experience deserves respect.

CONCLUSION

I believe that the main reason that explains the difference in impact between the top 5% of the digital talent in the world and the other 95% is as follows: The 95% inherit authorities from the industrial mindset, but the demand-driven economy that rules the market in our generation requires the ability to adapt quickly and to continuously satisfy your customer's needs. To build the right solutions, decisions should be made as close to the problem as possible, and in every decision, success should be defined and measured to be achieved. Empowered, inter-disciplinary, and symmetrical teams have the best chances of achieving this. Building successful digital products isn't possible through commoditized work: Motivated individuals driven by purpose make the difference.

Although segregating clear responsibilities makes people feel safe, that's just an illusion in most Product Development teams. This approach doesn't reflect the real level of uncer-tainty that should be managed, and the business ends up pay-ing a price, which then reduces the real level of safety for everyone. The 5%—successful Digital teams—work on shared ambitious objectives and make most product decisions driven by experiments. The power of embracing uncertainty is that we optimize for the case of being wrong, and that means that our failures are cheap. We validate our hypotheses in a way that everyone can validate the decisions, instead of blindly following some illuminated leader with an idea.

The irreverent way isn't for everyone: not everyone should stay on board for this journey, but the ones who stay will have the chance to live the most fulfilling career and maybe even life experience by being able to connect the activities they do every day with purpose and ambitious objectives. This is a journey of courage, requiring challenging authorities and deeply held beliefs. However, people who made this transformation not only created a positive impact in their careers, but also in their lives and even their families. Irreverents will never go back to working the way they used to work, because now they see a different approach that's effective, simple, and people-centric.

My mission, and the mission of this book, is to scale the impact of the 95% of digital talent by provoking a different understanding of product development and leadership.

If you'd like to learn more about the digital irreverent philosophy and become part of the community, kindly visit https://www.digitalirreverent.com.

Today we have enough access to knowledge and tools to leverage this mindset and significantly improve the world: We can create strong teams and build amazing products. I hope I can start to consider you an irreverent too. What can you do today to take the first step and drive your transformation?

REFERENCES

Beck, K. (1999). *Extreme programming: Embrace change.* Boston: Addison-Wesley Professional.

Cagan, M. (2008). *Inspired.* Silicon Valley: SVPG Press.

Christian, B & Griffiths, T. *Algorithms to live by: The computer science of human decisions.* London: Picador.

Doerr, J. (2018). *Measure what matters.* New York: Portfolio.

Gladwell, M. (2008). *Outliers: The story of success.* New York: Little, Brown & Co.

Hubbard, D. (June 2007). The IT measurement inversion. *CIO Enterprise Magazine,* https://www.cio.com/article/274975/it-organization-the-it-measurement-inversion.html.

Hubbard, D. (2014). *How to measure anything: Finding the value of intangibles in business.* Wiley, New Jersey.

Ismail, S., Malone, M. & van Geest, Y (2014). *Exponential organizations: Why new organizations are ten times better, faster, and cheaper than yours (and what to do about it).* New York: Diversion Books.

Kiyosaki, R. (1997). *Rich dad poor dad.* Scottsdale: Plata Publishing.

Maslow, A. (1943). A theory of human motivation: Psychological Review. 50(4), 370–396.

Royce, W. (1970). *How to implement large software systems.* IEEE WESCON (26, 328-388).

Scott, K. (2017). *Radical candor: Be a kick-ass boss without losing your humanity.* New York: St Martin's Press.

Sinek, S. (2016). *Most leaders don't even know the game they're in: Keynote from John C. Maxwell's Live2Lead event in Atlanta, Georgia, October 7, 2016.*

Sinek, S. (2020). *The infinite game: How great businesses achieve long-lasting success.* New York: Portfolio.

Takeuchi, H. & Nonaka, I (1986). *The new new product development game: Harvard Business Review.*

ABOUT THE AUTHOR

Uriel is a seasoned leader in the Technology and Product Development realm, renowned for his expertise in building and nurturing high-performing teams across Latin America and the Middle East. Uriel's career spans start-ups and large corporations with ambitious transformation goals, and he firmly champions the Lean Product Mindset as a core philosophy.

Uriel started his career in Argentina as a Software Engineer during the early years of Mercado Libre, the company that grew to become the largest e-commerce and payments platform in Latin America. He dedicated most of his fourteen years at Mercado Libre (Meli) leading Engineering and Product teams across the region and driving transformations in the acquisition of at least five companies. In his last assignment in Brazil, Uriel led the Developers Relations team and built a strong connection with the country's startup ecosystem.

Throughout his professional journey, Uriel has spearheaded digital solutions within industries that have experienced significant disruption, including e-commerce, urban mobility, and financial services, always promoting a people-centered approach and connecting business with technology at its core.

In the latest stage of his career, Uriel joined Edenred in UAE to help accelerate the financial inclusion in the region through the company's payroll and wallet solutions.

Beyond his corporate pursuits, Uriel is disciplined with his Yoga and meditation practices, is an avid enthusiast of crypto technologies, and also dedicates his time to mentoring young startups and offering his expertise to fellow leaders.

NOTES